JOSH WAITZKIN'S

ATTACKING ♟ CHESS ♟

AGGRESSIVE STRATEGIES AND INSIDE MOVES FROM THE U.S. JUNIOR CHESS CHAMPION

JOSH WAITZKIN,
INTERNATIONAL MASTER,
with Fred Waitzkin

A FIRESIDE BOOK
Published by Simon & Schuster
NEW YORK LONDON TORONTO SYDNEY TOKYO SINGAPORE

For my family.

FIRESIDE
Rockefeller Center
1230 Avenue of the Americas
New York, NY 10020

FIRESIDE and colophon are registered trademarks of Simon & Schuster Inc.

Designed by Stanley S. Drate/Folio Graphics Co., Inc.

Manufactured in the United States of America

10 9 8 7 6 5 4

Library of Congress Cataloging-in-Publication Data
Waitzkin, Josh.
    [Attacking chess]
    Josh Waitzkin's attacking chess : aggressive strategies and inside
  moves from the U.S. Junior Champion / Josh Waitzkin with Fred
  Waitzkin.
        p.   cm.
    "A Fireside book."
    Includes index.
    1. Chess.   I. Waitzkin, Fred.   II. Title.
  GV1449.5.W35   1995
  794.1'2—dc20   95-12178
                                                                        CIP

ISBN 0-684-80250-3

CONTENTS

ACKNOWLEDGMENTS

My love and gratitude to my mother, who contributed her experience as a chess teacher and her clarity of expression to this book. I am indebted to the efforts of John MacArthur, who spent long hours entering my early games into ChessBase, and to my friends Bruce Pandolfini, Maurice Ashley, and Gregori Kaidanov, who scoured the manuscript for errors. Also, for the inspiration of Jack, Neal, and Kitty.

Thanks, Dad, for teaching me how to write.

INTRODUCTION

I began playing chess at six years of age in Washington Square Park. My first opponents were chess hustlers, ex-cons, drug dealers, a homeless Russian chess genius, foul-mouthed gamblers, big jokers, and crafty tactical players who tried to lure passersby into a game for fifty cents or a dollar. Each one was an authority on chess. I remember those early games very well. I would plunk down in front of some guy five times my size and issue the challenge, "Wanna play?" I wanted to beat everyone. That was my earliest view of the game. We would begin to push our pieces ahead and I was instantly caught in the fear and thrill of battle. My objective was always rather simple: to attack and destroy. This was what the game was about. I was going to make threats, chop down his defenses, sacrifice pawns and pieces if I had to and then mate this big fella. For me chess was living on the edge, slugging it out, throwing material to the wind, giving mate. I recall bitter cold days in the park when sweat dripped down my sides as I battled some scary-looking dude across the board. I once said to my dad, "No sport makes me sweat as much as chess."

Throughout my career I've been known as a fierce attacking player, and this style has worked well for me. Since I was eight I have consistently been the top-ranked player in America for my age. Sometimes I see young players making listless moves, hanging back with their pieces, being cautious, settling for draws in winning positions, trying not to lose instead of playing aggressively to squash the enemy king. Frankly, I think that playing fearful drawish chess is a waste of time, but this stylistic malaise can plague even the bravest of competitors when they are slumping and short of confidence. There is a huge difference between wanting to slug it out and knowing how to do it. A young prizefighter with great heart will get knocked out again and again until he learns the science of boxing.

I think of myself as an aggressive person by nature. When I played for my high school basketball team I always looked to drive to the basket. In my classes in school I have never been shy about arguing my point of view. In chess, whether you see it as a game, art, sport, science, or a combination of these, your personality invariably has a large role in developing your playing style. When I first started playing the game at six I was pure aggression, trying to lay out my oversized opponents as if we were in physical battle. Noting my feisty early playing style and burning desire to win, my first coach and dear friend, Bruce Pandolfini, began to call me "Tiger." He still calls me "Tiger." This book is the chessic manifesto of an attacking mind. In life, would you prefer to be bold and adventurous or passive and fearful? I have always favored the former and I think this is the right approach for a chess player.

Needless to say, mothers have a slightly different view of most things. My mom recalls that when she watched me playing my first games she didn't see a wildcat so much as a little boy with an odd seriousness, as if her kid were inhabited by a wise old man. She says that there were afternoons when I played in the park with a steadiness and wisdom that seemed completely alien to the rough-and-tumble six-year-old who was her Josh.

Ho hum. Life is never simple. . . . But maybe I was both, the tiger and the old man. Chess is filled with paradox. It requires courage as well as patience. One must have rich imagination to complement cold calculation.

Whether tiger or old man, one thing is sure: when I was first sacrificing my pieces for mate in the park, and for years afterwards, I had little analytic understanding of what I was doing. In a sense the writing of this first book has been a form of self-discovery. Many of the rules and principles I discuss here were not taught to me but came intuitively through absorbing hard knocks in early games. In the beginning I did not understand these ideas concretely, but I played by them. Somehow I felt their essential correctness. I had a strange connection to the chessboard and its men, one that I will never truly understand.

The writing of this book has forced me to look analytically at what for the most part came naturally. It has been a trip into parts of my mind that I never bothered to consider. Perhaps because I am for the first time formulating key ideas in my chess life, these ideas will seem fresh and alive to you as they do to me. Some of these chapters were extremely difficult and frustrating to write. Time and again my father would read my drafts and say such things as "Josh, you never really explain why it is important to place rooks on the seventh" or "Why was that variation a blunder? You didn't explain it clearly." Having to explain what comes intuitively was infuriating and made me want to give up these words and go back to playing moves. I suspect that writing may be as difficult as chess.

I will demonstrate techniques of attacking chess from positions that I have chosen from my games. The positions will be arranged thematically and will tend to become more difficult as the book goes on. Through the use of diagrams and colloquial language I have tried to make even difficult ideas more accessible and human. When studying *Attacking Chess* I suggest that the reader stop whenever I ask a question. If possible, set the diagrammed position up on a chessboard, put the book down and don't pick it up until you have found what seems to be a solution. Try not to look ahead at the answer! When I first started to study chess, my father put tape over the answers so I wouldn't peek. Believe me, I know the temptation, but the lessons will hold more meaning if you earn them. Even if you cannot find a solution, struggle with the elements of the problem before reading my explanations. A willingness to accept the challenge of demanding material is half the battle.

I have broken the book down into various attacking themes, beginning with elementary ones such as forks, pins, and skewers, and moving progressively to more advanced and subtle ideas such as pawn storms, courage, don't settle for less, bust open the center, and zwischenzug. The moves are given in algebraic notation. If the reader is not completely comfortable with algebraic notation, an explanation is given in the appendix at the end of this book. The positions from my games illustrate key attacking ideas. Every analysis in this book is a chess lesson providing the student with numerous questions to study and answer as well as practical advice to digest. By the time you reach the concluding chapters of this work, most of the critical positions will require the employment of two or more attacking ideas. The most sophisticated and complex chess played in the world is a creative amalgam of the very ideas you will study here. In the final chapter of this book you will not be told in advance which themes must be employed to find the answers. Based upon what you have learned in the preceding pages, you will "feel" the moves and ideas much in the way that a strong player intuits critical moves in a beautiful game. By learning the manner in which key chess ideas grow out of one another, it is my hope that *Attacking Chess* will help to foster a player's creativity.

In addition to offering a teaching format culled from my games, and my best suggestions, I want *Attacking Chess* to be enjoyable reading. Good moves are combined with narrative accounts of experiences that I have had playing big games around the world. As a young veteran of many chess tournaments I can promise you that whether you are a thousand miles from home playing for first place in the final round of a world championship or at your local chess club facing a familiar rival in a weekend Swiss tournament, the theater of chess is as exciting as the moves themselves. Most chess books are dense with analysis and are relatively devoid of life. I believe that understanding the emotional turmoil of important chess games and hearing some of the wild and woolly stories surrounding tense chess rivalries will inspire the student of chess to study and improve his or her play.

Let's consider the short-lived but brutal rivalry of Waitzkin vs. Waitzkin. For the first two months of my chess life, my father and I played nearly every day. We had some terrific battles. Dad thought he was pretty good and in our games he never held back. Some afternoons he beat me three or four times and afterwards I felt numb. But by the next day, after school, I was ready to fight him again. We must have played a hundred games before I finally beat him. After that, our competition changed in almost every respect. I recall that after my first win Dad was thrilled . . . but this didn't last. For the next couple of weeks, as I began to win more often, he read chess books to get the upper hand. He was terribly proud of my chess ability, but at the same time he seemed frustrated. He didn't like losing to me. For my part, I didn't really want to play him so much anymore. I felt uneasy about checkmating my own father, but for an uncomfortable several weeks or so, we kept playing until he realized that this competition was not very good for either of us.

We would square off seated on the floor on opposite sides of a stubby-legged coffee table in the living room of our apartment. I couldn't quite reach all the way across the board and on long moves more often than not knocked over half the pieces. More than once, Dad suggested that I did this after he had built a winning position. Maybe this was so. For sure, Dad couldn't reconstruct the position once it was scrambled, and in those early games of my career I was at my wit's end trying not to lose.

Anyhow, at the time of the following game, I had turned the tables on Dad and was winning most of our games. By now he had become a little gun-shy. In this game he figured he'd play it safe and copy my moves — surely if his position were identical to mine nothing terrible would happen to him. Lots of beginners try the copycat strategy, but it is a critical error.

Here is the game: Waitzkin–Waitzkin, 1983. I was White.
**1.e4 e5 2.Nf3 Nc6 3.Bc4 Bc5 4.Nc3 Nf6 5.0-0 0-0
6.d3 d6 7.Bg5 Bg4 8.Nd5 Nd4 9.Nf6+ gf6 10.Bh6
Re8.** I had noticed that my father was copying my
moves up to this point, so I set a little trap. You might try
to find it.

Waitzkin–Waitzkin, 1983

WHITE TO MOVE:

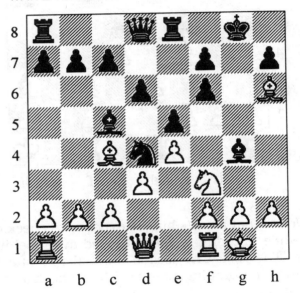

HINT: I figured that his predictability would persist and
his next two moves would be . . . Nxf3 and Bh3. The question to ask yourself is: how can I change my position so
that after he copies me I can take advantage?

I played **11.Kh1!** and he played right into my hands:
11 . . . Nf3 12.gf3 Bh3?

Now I used the small difference in the positions to win Black's queen. What did I play?

WHITE TO MOVE:

HINT: Notice that Black's king is exposed to check on the g-file, while my king is safely tucked away behind the h-pawn. The rook can escape the bishop's attack and check the king, gaining a tempo. Then, check and check to win the queen.

I played **13.Rg1+!** **Kh8 14.Bg7+ Kg8 15.Bf6+** (*discovered check*—the bishop has moved away exposing the king to the rook's attack. This is a double threat because the bishop is also attacking the black queen. We will look at these concepts again and again.) **15 . . . Kf8 16.Bxd8**, and White is up a queen. Soon after this my father and I stopped battling on the coffee table.

In my chess life my father moved very quickly from major rival to passionate coach. He had misgivings about our early slugfests and would be the first person to say that unless your little kid is very, very good, don't try to beat him every game. Chances are, repeated thrashings will kill his or her love for chess rather than kindle it.

As a coach, my father was terribly earnest about my early games, and I believe that this helped instill in me a sense for the importance of chess. When I was eight or nine and had suffered a bad defeat, he would not talk about chess moves. He would say to me things like, "You know, Josh, instead of looking at the game you were looking all around the room." Even today he watches my face and body English for clues about the quality of my focus. Before important tournaments we talk a lot about the kinds of things I must do to bring myself into top form, and afterwards we try to figure out what I might have done better: Did I study enough? Too much? Did I study the wrong material? Had I done enough physical training before the tournament? Had I slept enough? This, I believe, is the best way for a coach or a parent to help a young player. I am always appalled when I hear a frustrated dad scolding his four-foot son for playing queen to h6 instead of rook to a7. I wonder if that parent believes that he is helping his little warrior. His chess player will play brilliantly and make mistakes in the course of learning to attack and defend. It is the role of a parent to bring a healthy, well-rested child to the game, and then to focus on the psychological aspects of chess: to encourage good concentration, coolness under pressure, stamina, and patience to turn an advantage into a win. Sometimes a dad or mom should be no more than a shoulder to lean on, someone with a strong, fresh perspective. Life goes on. You win and you lose. You'll get 'em next time. Let's go get an ice cream cone.

1 MATE

This is what it's all about. As a six-year-old in Washington Square Park I didn't care about esoteric principles of strategic play. Terms like isolated pawn and opposite-colored bishops were irrelevant and absurd to me. I felt the game's artistic importance only in a vague, haunting fashion. My aesthetic appreciation for chess was not yet formed. My love for the game was fueled by a tremendous desire to win. My opponents were the bearded, warty, smelly, wrinkled fiends that haunted my darkest imaginings. Like a true-hearted superhero, I fearlessly threw my pawns, knights, and bishops at the enemy's castled position to open the way to the evil king. When the fearsome creature across the board resigned to my superior attack, I felt as mighty as a little boy looking for a place in this big world can feel.

It's been years since I delivered my first mates in Washington Square Park. Since then I have studied a lot of chess and my style as a player has evolved. Of course, I have had my ups and downs. During certain periods, particularly as a child, the right moves came magically to me, and I would win so many games that losing seemed impossible. Then there would be other periods when I would spoil all my winning positions, let my opponents wriggle off the hook. I can recall remarking in frustration, "I have forgotten how to win a game."

I think you will discover that each time you feel you have mastered this art, it slaps you on the wrist. That is part of the greatness of chess; it is impossibly complicated to master. Each time you think you have it, the game shows you that you are a mere beginner. When I was eleven years old, I drew a game against World Champion Garry Kasparov in a simultaneous exhibition. Later, I asked him to sign my chessboard. He thought for a minute and then wrote, "Good luck in the black and white jungle." At the time I didn't think much about it. But now I know that chess is a tumult of crazy deceiving vines and shadows, even for a genius like Kasparov.

How do we make our way through this jungle? There are so many ways to get lost. The same strategies that work so easily against beginners are repelled by intermediate players. The same endgame technique that ground out so many wins against national masters blows up in my face against grandmasters. Working to become more subtle and indirect as a player, it is easy to lose touch with fundamentals. Trying to become better, you can easily become worse.

Whenever I have trouble with my chess, I try to return to my roots as a player, my passion. I have to remember what first inspired me about the game, what I have always been good at. I am an aggressive competitor; I love to attack. The object of the attack is checkmate.

Let's examine some common mating setups. Probably the most common mating setup is the "support mate." This is when one piece defends another that checkmates the king from the square right next to him.

1

WHITE TO MOVE:

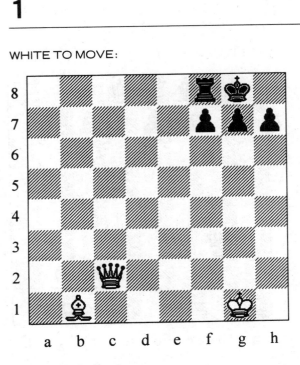

Checkmate in one move.

1.Qh7! mate. The queen is "protected" by the bishop on b1.

2

WHITE TO MOVE:

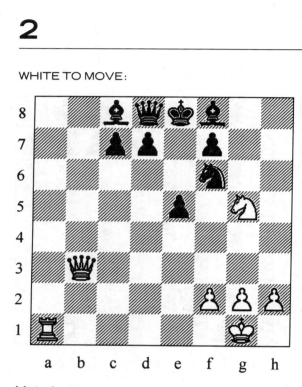

Mate in one.

1.Qf7! mate. The knight on g5 supports the queen.

The "back-rank mate" is another common setup. Often a king is trapped between the edge of the board and a phalanx of his own pawns. A check along the rank can prove decisive:

3

WHITE TO MOVE:

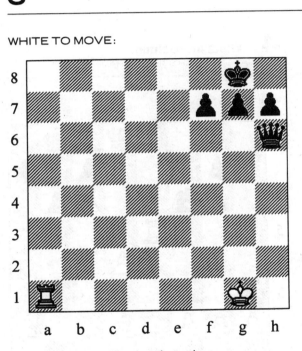

Checkmate on the back rank.

White wins with **1.Ra8 mate**.

Next is an example from one of my games. This position was reached in the fourth round of the 1992 National High School Championship. My opponent, a talented young player, is threatening to play Qxb2 checkmate. But it is my move. Here I used his back-rank weakness to force checkmate. Remember, I must check him at all times or else he will checkmate me. What should White play?

4 Waitzkin–Gelman

1992 NATIONAL HIGH SCHOOL CHAMPIONSHIP

WHITE TO MOVE:

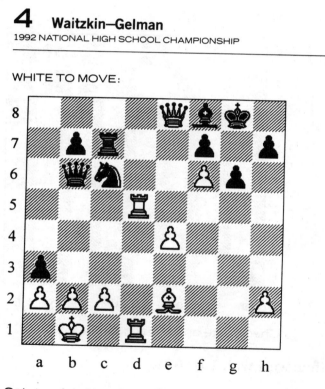

Set up a back-rank threat.

If you don't see the answer, take a look at the example above where the rook mates the trapped king. The pattern here is very similar. I played **1.Qxf8!+**. He has to take back, **1 ... Kxf8**. Suddenly I'm down a queen, but it doesn't matter. **2.Rd8+**. His king is checked and has nowhere to go, thanks to my rook and pawn on f6 and to his pawn on f7. He can take my rook, **2 ... Nxd8**, but after **3.Rxd8**, Black is in checkmate.

5

CHECKMATE:

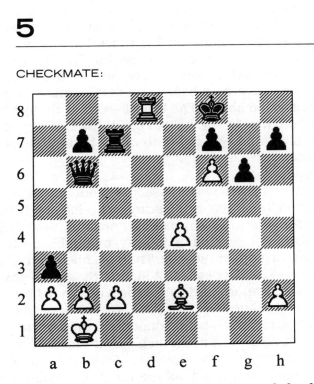

We can see from this example the power of the back-rank mate. A lone rook can catch the entire enemy army off guard. In this position all I have left is a rook and a bishop. He can even have my bishop if he wants it. Mate is all that counts.

Whether on the offense or defense, one should always keep an eye out for the back-rank mate. It is one of the most commonly overlooked traps in chess. I attended a small round robin tournament when I was nine years old where the players were all grandmasters. I watched one of the games closely. I was struck by the fact that many of their moves were so subtle that they made little sense to me. After several hours the game was very tense and complicated, with both of these powerhouse players building deep threats. I remember one grandmaster thinking on his move for fifteen minutes and then finally advancing his knight. His opponent walked across the room and, without even sitting in his chair, he delivered a back-rank mate similar to the one demonstrated above. The loser looked as though he had been punched in the belly. For all his brilliant, complicated plans, he had failed to allow breathing room for his king.

A very useful way to secure yourself from being mated on the back rank is to *make luft*, or breathing room, for your king. This can be done in the castled position, with a black king on g8, say, by pushing either the h- or g-pawn up one square. Then the check is harmless, as Kg7 or Kh7 is possible. Which of these two pawns to push is an important decision because they both create kingside weaknesses. As a little boy I always pushed my g-pawn until one strong opponent mated me with a queen on h6 and a knight on g5. Ever since, I have been careful about such weaknesses. Often it is the h-pawn that should be pushed, as the kingside remains rather secure. It should be noted that chess masters rarely create breathing space unless the back-rank threat is a real one. Each move in a chess game is precious. Giving away moves for no good reason is like throwing away money. If you give your opponent moves for free he will build his position with the extra time. When great players battle, even one wasted move may be a terminal mistake.

This one is a classical rendition: Two pieces combining to destroy royalty.

6

WHITE TO MOVE:

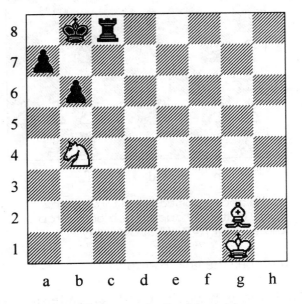

The minor pieces mate the black king.

1.Na6! mate. The white bishop takes away the a8 and b7 squares, and the knight hits the king and stops Kc7. The two attacking pieces are perfectly coordinated.

Next is a game of mine in which the same mating setup was used.

7   Altschuler–Waitzkin, 1985

WHITE TO MOVE:

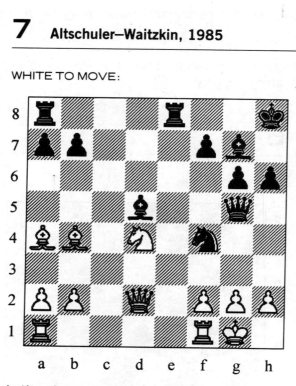

In the above position I am threatening Qxg2 mate. My opponent tried to stop the threat with **1.g3**. What did I play?

HINT: Remember the last example.

1 . . . Nh3! mate. It would have been better for White to stop mate with 1.f3, allowing the queen to defend along the second rank. Do you see what I had planned then?

8

BLACK TO MOVE:

After f3, the white queen guards g2.

HINT: Black should block the defense.

I was going to play 1 . . . Re2!!, blocking the defense along the rank. After 2.Qxe2 (if 2.Nxe2, Qxg2 is mate), 2 . . . Bxd4+ followed by capturing the queen wins a lot of material.

These last two positions showed a number of pieces combined in a well-coordinated attack. Later in the book we will study some more complicated forms of this type of mate. For now just appreciate the way the various pieces complement one another. Incidentally, I won a game in a speed chess tournament just a few weeks ago with the exact same mate.

The "smothered mate" is one of the nicest to execute. It involves a king being so totally locked in by his own pieces that a simple check will be decisive.

9

WHITE TO MOVE:

The lone knight kills.

1.Nd6 mate!

In 1988, when I was in the fifth grade, I reached the position below in the New York City Championships against Nicholas Proudfoot from the Hunter College Elementary School. I won the City Elementary Championship several times. Besides the National Championship, this tournament was the most important of the year for me. New York City has always had extremely talented scholastic players, and during the late eighties, this event, held at the Manhattan Chess Club, was particularly strong as some top young players from around the country traveled to the Big Apple to try their luck. It was funny having to compete against kids from Boston and Texas to win the city championship. This game against Proudfoot was a crucial one.

10 Proudfoot—Waitzkin

1988 NEW YORK CITY ELEMENTARY CHAMPIONSHIP

BLACK TO MOVE:

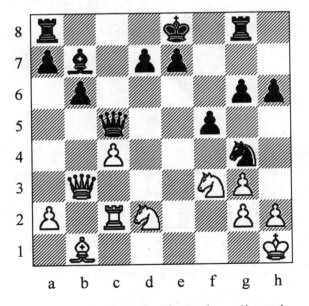

In this position I have a forced smothered mate in four! Take a little while and try to find it.

This is pretty difficult. If you see it, fantastic; if not, let's work a little closer to the critical position.

Correct is **1 . . . Nf2+ 2.Kg1 Nh3 double check**. The king is checked by my knight and by my queen on c5. The attack from the queen is known as a *discovery*, which will be dealt with in a later chapter. He played **3.Kh1**, as after 3.Kf1 I have the support mate 3 . . . Qf2 mate.

11

BLACK TO MOVE:

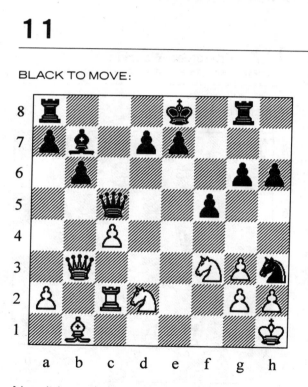

Now it is mate in two. Find Black's best move.

HINT: Remember I am setting up a smothered mate. If you still can't find the mate then try to envision how to make Nf2+ more powerful. In two moves this check will be mate!

I sacrificed my queen with **3 . . . Qg1 +**!! This would be a support mate except for **4.Nxg1**, and then I can decisively attack the smothered king with **4 . . . Nf2 checkmate**.

12

MATE:

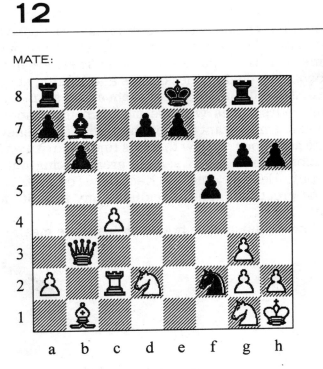

The white king is smothered.

In this game I gave up my queen to force one of White's men to trap his own king. My opponent hadn't seen 3 . . . Qg1+ because he wasn't so familiar with the various smothered mating setups. In fact, I had started to prepare this mate three or four moves before the position shown in the first diagram and was probably able to do so because I was already practiced at wielding the smothered mate. I particularly find the smothered mate aesthetically pleasing, as I am almost entirely using my opponent's pieces for my own ends.

It is useful to be familiar with the chess weapons; otherwise you will be reinventing the wheel over the board.

In the previous two examples I have just tried to give you a taste for mate, nothing more. There are of course numerous mating patterns in chess. There are hundreds of books devoted to checkmates and looking at some of these is useful practice. For a chessplayer, mate is the main course; it is why we sit down for dinner. As a player it is important to keep this in mind. Whenever my game goes sour, I know that it is time to turn away from positional subtleties. I sample great mating attacks of Morphy, Alekhine, Tal, and Kasparov. For me this is like eating great food, and it rekindles my appetite for the game I love.

Now we must learn how to prepare the meal.

2 THE FORK

Since the age of seven or eight I have looked forward to weekend chess tournaments as little vacations, a chance to drive to a new town or city, an excuse to spend the weekend in a nice motel with cable and pay-per-view. One spring when I was nine years old my dad scanned the tournament listings in *Chess Life* magazine and found an interesting "members only" tournament at the Franklin-Mercantile Chess Club in Philadelphia, one of the oldest chess clubs in the country.

On tournament weekends, our custom was to leave New York as soon as I finished school on Friday afternoon and take the football to throw around when we stopped for gas. When we arrived we would sometimes look for a movie, but more often we were both so excited about the tournament the next morning that we would hunt out the playing site, usually a church basement or a meeting room at a cheap motel or small college. We would say to one another that we wanted to check out the tables, to see what the room was like, but really we wanted to feel the excitement of the next day. We would convince ourselves that players would already be there, practicing, gearing up for the event, and of course I hoped to play a few speed games. Almost always, we would find a darkened church or a locked room, and a security guard who knew nothing about the tournament the following morning.

So this cold Friday night, we searched the deserted streets of downtown Philadelphia for the historic Franklin-Mercantile Chess Club with expectations of a brotherly reception. Except for a well-lit McDonald's on the corner, South 13th Street, where the club was then located, seemed to me a desert of shabby office buildings. I remember wearing a hood and gloves and shivering as we waited for someone to answer the doorbell. Across the street, several homeless people slept on a grating that steamed heat from an underground source. A surveillance camera checked us out in the lobby, and we felt pretty edgy as we entered the elevator. The chess club couldn't have looked less like a bustling tournament site. There were only a few stragglers reading tattered newspapers in the entryway, no wall charts or rows of chessboards on white cloth tables. Smoke hung in the air like a dense fog. A big man, 250 or 300 pounds, unshaven and reeking of Big Macs, challenged me to a five-dollar game. I was used to being lured into money games in Washington Square Park, where all sorts of hustlers tried out their luck. Normally I avoided gambling (my mother was adamant on this point) but I had come to this dank place to play chess, and if this was the way they initiated you in Philadelphia, so be it. My father gave me a nod, and we sat down to play. The big guy must not have been expecting much of a game and, to make a long story short, after I mated him he refused to pay the five dollars, which we wouldn't have taken anyway. That was my first game in the city of brotherly love.

I came to feel quite at home at the Franklin-Mercantile, and over the years I played in a half-dozen tournaments there. A sense of history was ingrained in the dark wooden tables. A love of chess hung in the air with the smell of stale french fries and Big Macs. The club inspired a kid to play his best.

When I was 12 years old I played the following game at a tournament for members of the Franklin-Mercantile.

In the diagrammed position I used a weapon that is one of the most fundamental tactical ideas in chess: the *fork*. You can imagine a fork in the road, a branching off. If one piece, say a knight or bishop, attacks two or more pieces at once, this is often sufficient to win material when only one piece can move or be defended.

13   The Fork

In diagram above the white knight is attacking Black's king, queen and rook, a triple fork! Any piece or even a pawn can be a good forker, but the knight is the most likely to fork because of its illogical pattern of moving. Again and again beginners overlook squares that are only one jump away for the knight. In Diagram 14 I set up a great fork.

14 Waitzkin–Clark, 1989

WHITE TO MOVE:

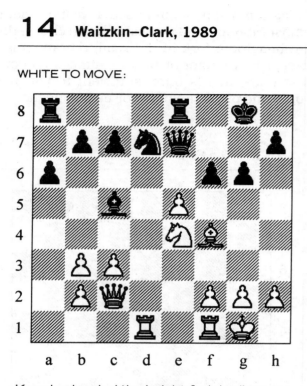

Keeping in mind the knight fork in diagram 13, what do you play?

HINT: You will notice that the black queen and knight defend the f6-pawn, which is, in turn, attacked by White's e-pawn and by the knight on e4. If the black knight were gone, White could take the pawn with check, winning the rook. And better yet, if another piece were on the d7 square we could have a potential three-way fork!

I played **1.Rxd7!** and my opponent resigned because he realized that after 1 . . . Qxd7, 2.Nxf6+! wins the queen.

Another attacking theme illustrated in this position is *removing the defender.* The black knight was guarding the f6-pawn, so we simply got rid of it. We will explore this concept in detail later.

When you become increasingly familiar with the knight's movements the forking setups will become more apparent. A few rules of thumb might be helpful.

1. If your opponent's knight defends a square or a piece that you are attacking with a knight of your own, once the defender is removed (in this case my rook removed the knight and the queen took back) and your knight reaches the targeted square (f6), it will also eye the square of the removed defender. This rather long-winded but simple idea is crucial to the above example.
2. The knight has a logic of its own. Unlike all other pieces, it does not move in straight lines. If you sit down with an empty chessboard and a knight and you move it around a bit, you might start to see some patterns. The most basic is that a knight must move from a dark square to a light square and so on. It can never go light to light or dark to dark.

Put a black knight on e4 of your chessboard. Now see which squares around the knight are the hardest for it to reach.

15 Knighttime

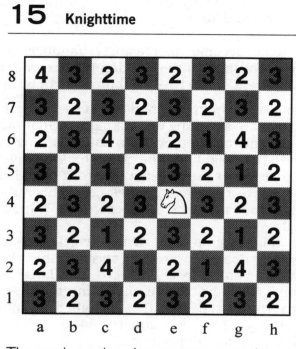

The numbers show how many moves the knight on e4 needs to make to reach each square on the board.

You discover quickly that the knight's sense of distance is at first unpredictable and weird. The knight needs three moves to reach e5, d4, e3, or f4, squares right next to him. Squares located diagonally adjacent to the knight, d3, d5, f5, or f3, are only two moves away. Now consider the squares located diagonally from the knight only two squares away: c6, c2, g2, g6. It takes four moves for the knight to get there!

Return for a moment to diagram 13 with this idea in mind. The knight is threatening the Qd7 and Re8 but is four moves away from the square right between them: d8! The understanding of these relationships is of huge importance. For example if you are playing speed chess it is often handy to be as "far away" from an aggressive knight as possible. Strong players also use this knowledge to quickly calculate the timing and validity of middlegame maneuvers. I would suggest taking a few minutes and trying to really gain a grasp of the above diagram.

Remember to look not only for forks of your own, but also for those of your opponent. Until you are familiar with the odd L-shaped movement of the knight, its fork can be an unexpected and cruel surprise. This can be safely said about the entire arsenal of weapons you will need to master to build deadly attacks. The greatest attacker will fail if he is heedless of the threats of his opponent. While we learn to attack, we also must learn what to look out for in defense.

The feel of the fork, and the feel of the movements of the knight, will come with time (and work). There are hundreds of books crammed with tactical exercises, including knight forks. The student of chess must invest some time studying such examples.

PINS AND SKEWERS

3

When a wrestler is pinned to the mat it is a moment of total helplessness; he cannot move. It is a moment when he may wish that some kind soul would offer a helping hand, get this sweaty hulking creature off him. Alas, freedom will only come at the price of loss of the match. A pinned chess piece often finds itself in a similar bind—down for the count—unless a friend can come to his aid in the nick of time.

16 Pins

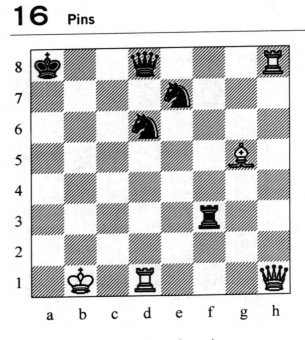

All of Black's pieces are pinned.

Note how the various pins are constructed. The rook on f3 can't move legally because the white queen has pinned it to the black king. Neither knight wants to move because of the pins by the rook on d1 and the bishop on g5. The black queen is pinned to the king by the rook on h8. In short, Black is in a lot of trouble. Now let's see a more practical example:

17

BLACK TO MOVE:

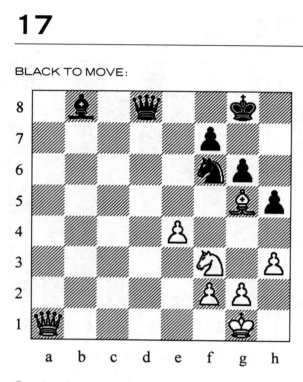

Can he save the knight on f6?

The black knight is pinned. If it were to move, White could respond by taking the black queen: Bxd8. The only ways that Black can hope to break the pin are to

1. Dislodge the white bishop, which will prove very difficult in this position.
2. Move the queen off the dangerous diagonal to d6 and thus free the knight.
3. Maneuver the black bishop to e7 to block the potential attack on the queen.

But Black has an immediate problem here: White is threatening the knight twice and therefore the immediate Qb6 or Qd6 doesn't work. The only reasonable move for Black is **1 . . . Kg7**. But now the poor knight is pinned two ways. The process of freeing the unfortunate fellow will be painstaking and ultimately futile. If time allowed, Black would have to first play Qb6 to defend the knight and get off the diagonal. Then he must maneuver the bishop to d8 or e7 in order to protect the knight a second time and make possible Kh7 to get off the white queen's pin. Then Black would be able to move his poor knight again. Unfortunately, he will not have time for this saving maneuver.

18

WHITE TO MOVE:

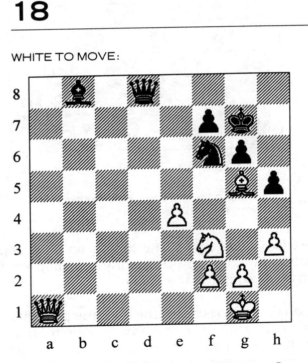

After Kg7, what is White's winning move?

Correct is **2.e5!** and the knight falls. Attacking the pinned piece is devastating.

19 Waitzkin–Russo

1985 GREATER N.Y. PRIMARY CHAMPIONSHIPS

WHITE TO MOVE:

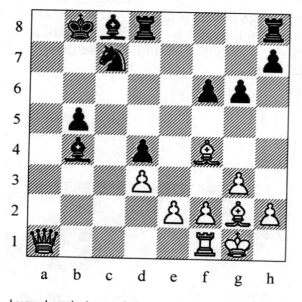

I used a pin to end the game in this position. Find mate in one.

Correct is **1.Qa8!** mate. The knight on c7 is rendered absolutely immobile by the pinning bishop on f4. My bishop on g2 supports the queen.

Next is a more recent game than the previous ones. I was sixteen years old and my opponent was a very strong Russian-American grandmaster. Alexander Ivanov is known internationally to be a powerhouse GM with one glaring flaw: He always gets into *time pressure*.

In tournament chess, players have to make a certain

number of moves within a time limit, for example, thirty moves in ninety minutes (30/90). After completing the required moves, the player receives additional time for more moves and so on. If the flag falls (mechanical chess clocks have a flag that falls when the minute hand reaches twelve) before the required moves are completed, you lose.

All players occasionally get into time pressure and must rush to complete the required moves. Sometimes we fall into the beauty of our thoughts and lose all sense of the clock. Sometimes the position has been too complex to understand in the allotted time. In a very dangerous position, it is sometimes better to find the right move than to worry about the clock.

But for some players, time pressure becomes an addiction: the game is not complete without the rush of emotion that comes when they must make a half-dozen critical moves in eight or ten seconds. Ivanov, for example, is a marvelous speed player but always plays his tournament games much too slowly. At the end of each of his games, a group of fans gathers around his board as the grandmaster shakes and quivers and grimaces while reeling off twelve or fifteen or even twenty-five moves without an instant to think. I am always afraid Ivanov will have a heart attack in time pressure: just to watch him is nerve-wracking.

Anyway, back to pins. In the next diagram, predictably, Ivanov is in big time pressure with one move to make before his flag falls. It is my move now and I have a very good one that is made possible by an excellent pin. In fact I had seen this idea four or five moves earlier and had been setting it up.

20 GM Alexander Ivanov–Waitzkin

1993 NEW YORK OPEN

BLACK TO MOVE:

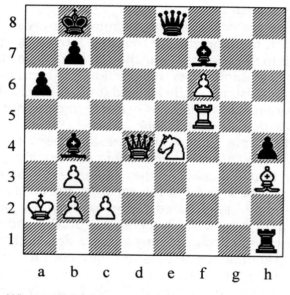

What can Black do now?

HINT: It's what chess is all about.

I played **1 . . . Qa4 checkmate!** It is not often that you get to blindside a GM with mate in one. He can't take my queen because of the pin by my bishop on f7. Here we can fully appreciate the power of the pin. At first glance White's king looks pretty secure. In effect, though, the b3-pawn doesn't exist! If a grandmaster can overlook a pin like this, imagine how useful a tool it will be to understand!

We have seen from these examples how a pin can freeze a piece. The best way to go about taking advantage of a pinned piece is to either attack it again or to attack what the pinned piece once defended. After all, a guard with no legs will not do much good.

You may have noticed that in all of the above examples a less valuable piece was pinned to one of more importance. It is for this reason that it can't move. The skewer, geometrically quite similar to the pin, is more compelling, because the larger piece is the one being attacked immediately and the lesser piece will come under direct fire once the other one moves. For this reason it is more powerful, more forcing, "mandatory" as my mother would say.

21

WHITE TO MOVE:

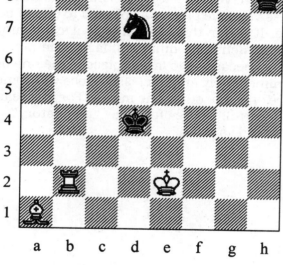

Form two skewers.

1.Rd2 double check and two black pieces come under fire.

22 Waitzkin–Ruch

1985 GREATER N.Y. PRIMARY CHAMPIONSHIP

WHITE TO MOVE:

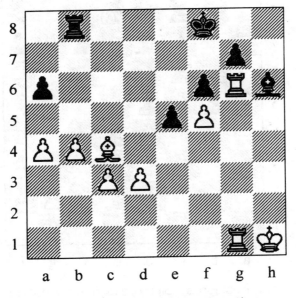

I reached this position against Jonathan Ruch, who would later be my teammate at the Dalton School. How can I set up a skewer?

HINT: It involves a sacrifice.

I played **1.Rxh6!** and after **1 . . . gxh6 2.Rg8+**, skewering his king to his rook, **2 . . . Ke7 3.Rxb8**, and I netted a piece and went on to win easily.

23 Waitzkin–Langlois, 1987

WHITE TO MOVE:

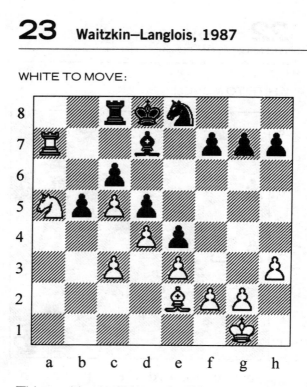

This position is a bit more difficult. What do you think White should play?

HINT: I sacrificed to set up a skewer, after which I would win a pawn.

1.Rxd7+! Kxd7 2.Bg4+, skewering his king to the rook.

24 The king is skewered!

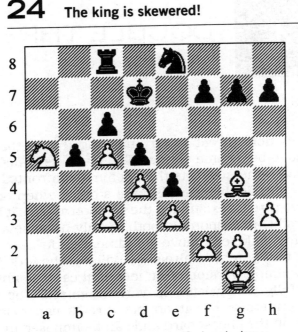

After the king moves out of check, how does White win material?

2 . . . Kc7 3.Bxc8 Kxc8 4.Nxc6! The whole point of the combination was to remove his defense of the c6-pawn. I went on to win the endgame.

You can see how skewers (and other tactics) can be set up by sacrifices. The only three pieces that can skewer or pin in chess are the bishop, queen, and rook. This is because no other pieces can move distances in straight lines. The pin hits the weaker piece first and X-rays the stronger piece. The skewer sets an immediate threat to the stronger piece and thus forces it to move, exposing an attack upon the weaker piece.

DOUBLE THREAT

The double threat is an attacking theme that often proves to be a game winner. The name itself defines its character and suggests the dilemma confronted by the victim of a double threat. Quite simply, when one side has two threats existing in the position at once it is often impossible to respond to both, if only because a player can only make one move at a time. One form of double threat that you have already studied is the fork. This is a very simple version of an idea that can be subtly and beautifully constructed in various guises. The reader must understand that double threats can exist anywhere on the chessboard and can be imposed by different pieces.

25

WHITE TO MOVE:

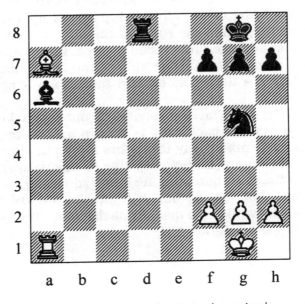

White is down a piece here and must win
one back to save the game.

At first glance the white rook appears to be threatening the black bishop on a6. But look more closely. This is not a real option because of White's weakness on his back rank. Although the black bishop on a6 is hanging, White cannot play 1.Rxa6 because of 1 . . . Rd1, a back-rank checkmate. With this in mind, do you see a way that White can set up a double threat?

HINT: How can you give your king breathing space? In other words, which move renders Black's rook d1+ harmless by simply allowing White to stroll his king away?

The correct move is **1.h4!** Look at this for a moment. This move, amazingly, threatens Rxa6! Take a minute and make sure you understand why. After Rd1+ White can simply and happily play Kh2. Because of 1.h4, there is no longer a back-rank weakness! Now the double attack should be clear. White's h-pawn is attacking the black knight, while the rook on the a-file threatens the black bishop. Black must lose a piece. Can you believe that a move so far on one side of the board, and by a pawn, such a little soldier, can have such a powerful effect?

You'll recall that the device of moving a kingside pawn to free the back rank is known as "making luft." The most common way to do this is by pushing the h-pawn one square, as typically this is less weakening in the middlegame than pushing it two squares.

Notice that 1.f4?, although it attacks the knight and makes luft, would be a disastrous decision. Try to figure out why. (See Diagram 26.)

26

BLACK TO MOVE:

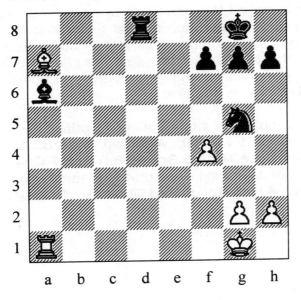

How can Black undo White's last attempt to create a double attack with a single move?

1.f4 creates a double threat to be sure; the only problem is that Black can defend against both of them with 1 . . . Ne4! The knight is no longer attacked and the white king's breathing room is taken away once again as the f2 square is covered. 2.Rxa6 is impossible once more because of Rd1 mate. White must take the time to make room for his king by pushing another of his kingside pawns and meanwhile Black will move his bishop. Black will be able to retain his extra piece, which is an overpowering advantage.

This example has shed light on the flexibility of the double threat. We should notice that even innocuous-looking chess moves can have a powerful bite. Watch out for them. We have also gotten another glimpse of the importance of the back rank. A final lesson can be taken from the move 1.f4? Sometimes two moves that look the same can be quite different. The ability to find the best move is of utmost importance. A lazy chess player might think, "h4, f4, they do the same thing, no problem." A strong chess player will look for the difference, find it, and play the correct move.

Let's look at a game I played against a 1605-rated player when I was ten years old. **1.d4 d5 2.c4 dc4 3.Nf3 Nf6 4.e3 Bg4 5.Bc4 e6 6.0-0 c5 7.Qa4+ Nc6?** This move is a mistake and now I can jump into the driver's seat. **8.Ne5 Rc8 9.Bb5 Qb6?**. (See Diagram 27.)

27 Waitzkin–Kurtovic, 1987

NORTHEAST CHESS CONGRESS UNDER-1900

WHITE TO MOVE:

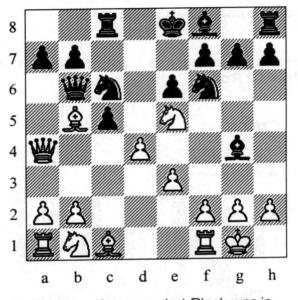

Qb6 was another error, but Black was in trouble anyway. Now find how White can use a double threat to win material.

HINT: Open up a crucial rank.

The correct move is **10.dxc5!** threatening the black queen and opening up the white queen's path to the g4-bishop.

The game went **10 . . . Bxc5 11.Bxc6+!** (essential or else the bishop will hang when my queen leaves to capture on g4.) Then **11 . . . bxc6 12.Nxg4 Nxg4 13.Qxg4**, and I have won a piece thanks to a neat double threat. Notice also the theme of *discovered attack* in this tactic: dxc5 uncovered the threat of the queen to the bishop on g4. In a later chapter we will study discoveries in more depth.

The game continued: **13 . . . 0-0 14.Nc3 Rfd8 15.b3 Bb4 16.Bb2 Rd2.**

28

WHITE TO MOVE:

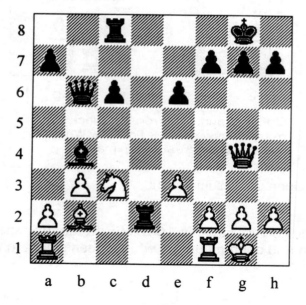

Here I used a final double threat and he resigned. Can you find it?

HINT: The theme of discovery, the uncovering of a sheltered threat by moving another pawn or piece out of the way, is used once again. There are two answers.

I played **17.Na4!** and he resigned, as I was both threatening his queen and 18.Qxg7 checkmate (I opened up my b2-bishop's diagonal). Do you see the other move?

17.Nd5! does the same thing. If 17 . . . cxd5 18.Qxg7 mate, and if 17 . . . Rxb2 18.Nxb6 wins the queen. Only one threat at a time can be answered.

These two examples have shown how simple moves can prove decisive. When pawns open up the lines for their pieces, all hell breaks loose. The student of chess will soon discover that basic themes, such as discoveries, forks, pins, etc., combine to yield positions that are interesting and almost infinitely subtle. The greatest players in the world build upon the basics that we are studying here.

REMOVING THE DEFENDER

In the following lesson I will discuss a position that I arrived at in the next to last round of the 1989 New York State Junior High School Championship. My opponent was Eric Smith, a talented and aggressive young player. Each of us had won our four previous games and we both knew that the state championship was likely to go to the winner of this one. As is often the case between young rivals, there wasn't too much good blood between Eric and me. In fact, I can't remember looking at him when he didn't seem to scowl back; perhaps I did the same. There was hostility here, but then again there is a built-in antagonism between all competitors. The trick for a chessplayer is to not get caught up in anger to the extent that judgement is impaired. This is especially difficult for young players. The deeper trick is to take hostility and channel it into inspired play. Garry Kasparov, the World Champion, is brilliant at taking negative emotions and transforming them into tremendous energy at the board.

This game was big for both of us. With the black pieces, Eric chose to play the Dragon Sicilian, an opening given its name because the pawn structure resembles the figure of a sleeping dragon. This setup was also one of my early weapons when I had black, because the challenge of a tactical duel was always welcome. It is a dangerous opening riddled with tactical intricacies and wild complications.

Middlegames that arise out of the Dragon Sicilian often come down to a crazy race with White attacking on the kingside and Black attacking on the queenside. Whoever is faster to force mate will be the victor. The players, even if they are grandmasters, seem to be disregarding their opponent's moves, attacking heedlessly. The Dragon—the very name suggests ferocity—has been the battleground for many brilliant contests and has baffled the greatest players for years.

In this game my attack was more successful than my opponent's and his position is dire. As you learn the rules of aggressive play you will also learn to keep a watchful eye on your own king even while unleashing your own mating attack. The king is, after all, indispensable. In most chess games defense is an aspect of attack. It is often essential to hold off an assault for a tempo or two in order to give yourself time to deliver the crushing move. You will notice, for instance, in the position below, that my rook on h2 both pressures the h-file and horizontally defends the c2-pawn. This serves as a valuable defense, stalling my opponent's queenside attack. White's position here is dominant, and the time has come to deliver the final blow.

29   Waitzkin–Smith

1989 NEW YORK STATE JR. HIGH SCHOOL CHAMPIONSHIP

WHITE TO PLAY:

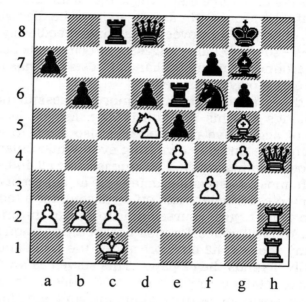

My opponent thought all was well, as his bishop guards the h8 square and his knight protects h7. But look a little deeper, and remember that I have three powerful pieces on the critical h-file. How does White win?

HINT: If you see the answer, that's great. If not, I will talk you through it. One important thing a player must understand is that although the queen is the most powerful piece on the board, she is not the king and her loss is not the end of the game. Beginners sometimes forget that they can give up the queen for mate.

Did you analyze **1.Qh8+!**? Immediately, of course, you noticed that Black would respond with **1 . . . Bxh8**, and suddenly you are down a queen, but there is more because you still have two warriors on the h-file. After **2. Rxh8, Kg7** is forced. You may have calculated this far and not seen what to do, because if the rook on h1 checks the king on h7, Nf6xg7 and Black is winning. 4.Rxd8, capturing the queen, is not very good because after Black recaptures 4 . . . Rxd8, the attack is over and Black is *up the exchange* with White's rook, bishop, and knight against Black's two rooks and knight. The position after 2 . . . Kg7 is the crucial one to visualize. What can I play here?

30

WHITE TO MOVE:

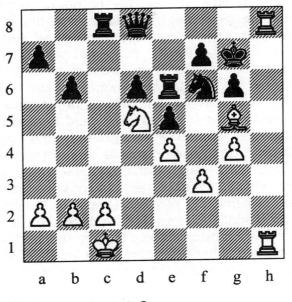

What prevents mate?

HINT: The knight on f6 prevents mate, of course. So now think what White can play to *remove the defender* without allowing Black to escape.

3.Bxf6+! The knight is gone and it is check! (Taking on f6 with the knight doesn't work because it is without check. Black's queen can defend by capturing the rook on h8). **3 . . . Rxf6** is forced, and now the path is clear. **4. R1h7** mate. This calculation might seem very difficult but with some work it shouldn't be so hard to see. It was probably the side move Bxf6+ that my opponent hadn't noticed. Slightly away from the main line of attack, this removes the defender and allows White to mate.

What did we learn from this example? First, and perhaps most importantly, we learned how necessary it is to control anger we may feel toward an opponent. This is sometimes hard to do but is very essential. Anger can cloud your vision as a chess player, not to mention as a human being. Psychology is a major element in the game of chess, as it is in all sporting competitions. Top players are always looking for psychological advantages to go along with good moves. There are numerous little tricks employed to annoy one's opponent, and some are quite primitive. For example, one strong junior who had recently immigrated from Russia would shake the table with his knees whenever we were in a time scramble. I can tell you that my anger at this dumb ploy was more destructive to me than the shaking table. I began to hate this kid, which I believe was exactly what he wanted. Instead of seeing the position clearly and objectively I would be muddled by my intense desire to rip this guy up. One time he hung a piece against me, and, wanting to beat him so badly, I never noticed. In the above game I could feel that Eric wanted to crush me. Perhaps his anger colored his calculation.

More technically, the idea of combining attack with defense was key in the Smith game. Recall the rook on h2 eyeing two separate fronts: protecting my weak pawn on c2 and attacking the open h-file. We saw that queens are not indispensable, that a barrage of pieces can be very powerful, and sometimes a sacrifice is necessary to realize an advantage. The theme of *removing the defender* came into play here. This is a crucial idea. Ask yourself the question: What prevents mate? Is it the knight? So get rid of it.

6 DISCOVERY

You are reading a book. It is the most exciting moment in the story. The hero has braved epic storms crossing the Pacific in a small sailboat to reach his long-lost love and is now battling starvation . . . when your phone rings. The phone call is boring, irrelevant. You speak politely, an old friend drones on. You are between worlds. Finally you manage to get off, but then the book seems to have disappeared. Romance is fading. You can't believe that this has happened to you. You're a wreck and are searching frantically everywhere. You lift a pillow on your bed, and there it is. Now that is a welcome discovery. Only on the chessboard, instead of moving a pillow to find J. D. Caldwell's *Desperate Voyage*, you move a pawn or a piece to uncover an attack. In more chessic language, a "discovery" or "discovered attack" is the movement of one piece so a blocked line of attack is now exposed.

The following position is from a game I played in the fourth round of the 1990 National Elementary Championships in Tucson, Arizona. My thirteen-year-old imagination was churning with discoveries, and I went on to win this tournament. Consider Diagram 31 as a lesson rather than a problem.

31 Waitzkin–Valente

1990 NATIONAL ELEMENTARY CHAMPIONSHIPS

WHITE TO MOVE:

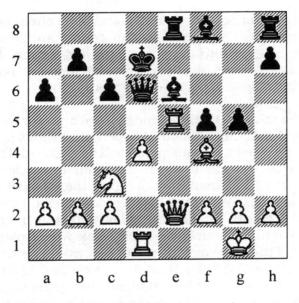

Let's walk through this one.

It is White's move. One potential discovery is to move the rook on e5, exposing an attack from the f4-bishop on the black queen on d6. This cannot be done now, however, because the bishop is attacked by the pawn on g5. If White tries to play 1.Rd5 with the idea of a double attack on the queen while she is pinned by the rook to the king, Black has 1 . . . Bxd5!, exposing a discovery of his own: 2.Bxd6 Rxe2!, and White is in trouble. Remember that often in chess the threat is stronger than the execution. The idea of this discovered attack is menacing but at the moment it does nothing but haunt Black and restrict his possibilities. Later the effect will be more tangible.

My correct move here will be more accessible to the reader after studying the next few chapters. Still, what do you think I should play?

HINT: A very important axiom of attacking chess is that if your opponent's king is in the center and you have strong central development, *open the center*. An advanced player will feel the correct move in this position: there is no need to calculate very far.

The best move is **1.d5!** opening all the lines for the white pieces. When the d-file bursts open, the tender positioning of the black king and queen will be exposed. The conclusion of the game is an excellent example of the discovery: **1 . . . cxd5** (if 1 . . . gxf4, then 2.dxe6+ wins the queen because of the discovered attack on the black queen) **2.Nxd5**. Holding the possibilities in the air. If I had recaptured with my e-rook Black would play 2 . . . Bxd5 and the discovery on my queen would be very bad. If 2.Rd-d5 Bxd5 3.Rxe8, then 3 . . . gxf4 and Black is up a piece. It's amazing how difficult this game is; Black's position is terrible, but one slipup and he will win.

32

BLACK TO MOVE:

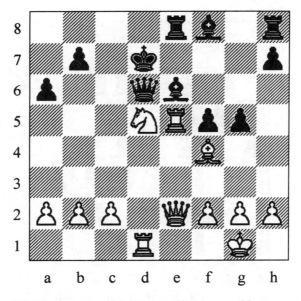

White must have a threat, because I have ignored my f4-bishop *en prise*. Can you find it?

My threat is Nb6+ or Nf6+ with, yes, a discovered attack on the black queen. If Black takes the knight with 2 . . . Bxd5, then I win with 3.Rdxd5 Rxe5 4.Qxe5! Black, after 2.Nxd5, played **2 . . . Kc8!** Now if White moves his knight to f6 with a discovery on the black queen it is pretty good, but it is still more effective to hold back. The threat is menacing but the execution would not yet be deadly. White can continue the attack with **3.Qc4+!** If 3 . . . Kb8, then White can play Rxe6, winning the queen. (Make sure you understand why.) If 3 . . . Kd8 then 4.Rxe6

Qxe6 5.Qc7+ + is checkmate. So Black must play **3 . . . Qc6**.

33

WHITE TO MOVE:

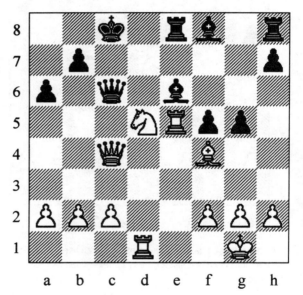

It might seem as if Black has gotten out of danger, but White is ready to set up a fatal discovery.

4. Nb6+! The black queen is pinned and cannot capture the white knight because of the white queen's attack on the black king. The only legal moves for the black king put him on the deadly path of White's dark-squared bishop. After **4 . . . Kc7**, what do you find for White?

   5. Rxe6+! Another discovered check attacking the

pinned queen. If Black captures the checking bishop with 5 . . . gxf4, I take the queen with my rook on e6. My opponent blocked the check with **5 . . . Bd6**, then **6. Bxd6+**, and Black is nearly finished. His only move is **6 . . . Kxb6**.

34

WHITE TO MOVE:

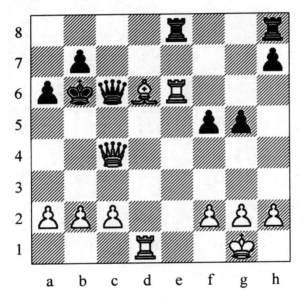

How do we win the black queen now?

HINT: Discovery.

I continued with **7.Bc5+! Kc7**. (7 . . . Qxc5 is illegal because of the rook on e6.) Now is the moment to take the queen. **8.Rxc6+**, and my opponent played **8 . . . Kxc6**.

Black is finished, although 8 . . . bxc6 would have been better. Now White can deliver a blow that fits thematically with the whole attack.

35

WHITE TO MOVE:

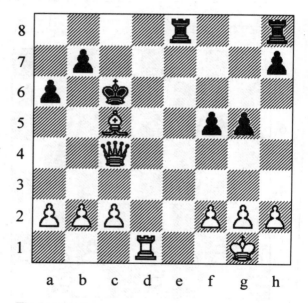

Find mate in one.

Yes, there are two answers here. 9.Ba7 and the move I played, **9.Be3 discovered checkmate!**

You must see the power of the discovery from this game. Again, this was not an example in which you were supposed to see all the moves. Just learn from the rhythm of the attack, feel it. Each time you learn a new idea it is a building block. In some future game it will come in handy. More importantly, each new idea seems to lead to another breakthrough, and so on. The house grows stronger and taller. In the above game the unraveling of Black's position began with my decision to delay utilizing my discovered attack. Initially it would not do much, and I felt that the opening up of the position would make my threats really work. Also, an interesting relationship to keep in mind is that if a rook is lined up on the same file as the enemy queen it is favorable for the rook and is a good file to open up.

What did we learn? 1. The power of the discovery. 2. Don't rush to use all your weapons. Earlier I could have used the discovery but I didn't see a forced win. 3. Perhaps the most important lesson to be learned from this example was that of the first move. You will begin to feel when to open the position. 1.d5! was a crucial thematic central break that made all of the fancy tactics possible. If you are more prepared in a certain area or your opponent's king is exposed, the time may be right to *open the position*. This theme will be discussed in a more focused manner in the next few chapters.

7 BUST

There is a moment in any attack where quiet moves are no longer appropriate. All attacks build to a critical moment. This is the point in the game where the aggressor must the seize the day. The required move may well be a bold one and entail some risk. Checkmate is, reasonably, the hardest thing to do in a chess game, so it is essential that a player be willing to take risks in order to achieve that goal. Again and again in chess we see examples of players achieving winning positions and then wimping out at the very moment that a mortal blow is called for.

Consider Diagram 36: I reached this position in 1989 against Marc Berman, a teenage rival against whom I had squared off in many tough battles.

36 Waitzkin–Berman, 1989

WHITE TO MOVE:

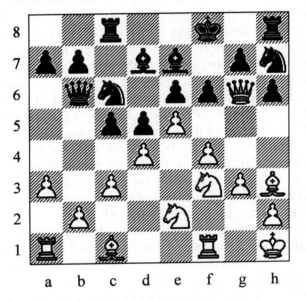

In the above position Black is in trouble. His king is clearly not very happy, and it is questionable whether his pieces are doing anything useful. Still, the game has to be won and so I ask you to come up with White's best move.

HINT: Recall the first move of the last chapter.

My best is **1.f5!** Make this move on your chessboard. Your first reaction might be that the position is just too complicated for you to calculate. This might very well be true and I probably didn't see all the possible consequences of the move when I played it. Positions involving this type of pawn tension are tremendously difficult to calculate, as the whole board seems to be on the verge of exploding. Chessic explosions are thrilling but they are also scary. As a player it is quite easy to fall into a pattern of making timid choices, but if you avoid moves that entail risk you will surely lose out on experiencing the high art in the game.

Why 1.f5? This brings us to one of the most beautiful and mysterious elements of chess: *feeling*. In the game I felt that the position required this move and I trusted my instincts. Let's look at factors that might have guided my intuition. My queen is near the enemy king, who can never castle away. This is good but will not do much unless I can get some more of my pieces to help in the attack. But how to do that? Imagine if all of the f- and e-pawns were gone. Black would be finished, as the black king would be completely deserted and vulnerable to any attack: my rook on f1, for instance, would become a monster ramming down his throat.

If we understand this idea of destroying the center and kingside barriers, the move is quite easy. I want the whole board to explode! No matter how Black responds, lines will open up, and this can only help me.

Think of it this way: If you are attacking a vulnerable king on any side of the board, open up that side! Remove the pawns from the defense. Sometimes this will involve a sacrifice, as in the next example, and sometimes a move like f5 will be necessary.

Now let's look at the end of the game to feel the power of *busting open the kingside*. My opponent played 1 . . . **Ng5**. There are many different alternatives, as I mentioned above, all of which are favorable for White. The game continued: **2.Nxg5 hxg5 3.exf6 Bxf6 4.fxe6 Be8**. Find my next thrust.

37

WHITE TO MOVE:

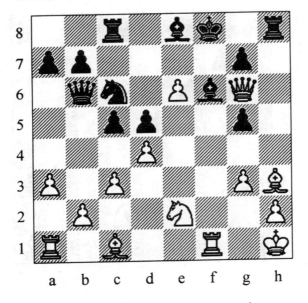

Winning a "won game" in chess can be
quite difficult and entails imagination.

Here we have reached another critical moment in the
attack. The defense is nearly all broken down, but I still
must find critical moves to win! Compare this diagram
with the last. Using the knowledge you have just gained,
how do you think I should continue?

Remember, breaking into the kingside often involves
a sacrifice. **5.Rxf6 + !** and poor Black is running out of
defenders. **5 . . . gxf6 6.Qxf6+ Kg8 7.Qxg5+ Kf8**.
There is one more interesting position from the Berman game:

38

WHITE TO MOVE:

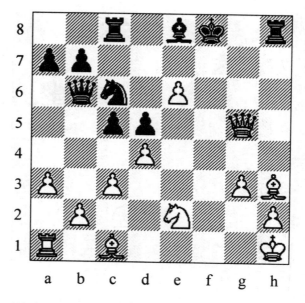

We have been successful in stripping Black's defense down to the bone. But what now? There should be a mate, now only to find it.

Think . . . maybe I need to bring one more piece into the attack.

Here I played a relatively quiet and completely decisive move. I simply completed my development with **8.Be3!!** This plans the entrance of my final rook into the attack via f1. There will be a chapter later on the insidious creature known as the *quiet move in attack*. Black can do nothing now. The game finished **8 . . . Bh5 9.Rf1+ Ke8 10.Qg7**, and Black resigned because of my double threat of Qd7 mate and Qxh8.

We just saw an example in which I used pawns to bust open my opponent's kingside. Now let's check out a position in which a piece does the dirty work.

39 Waitzkin–Khurgin, 1989

WHITE TO MOVE:

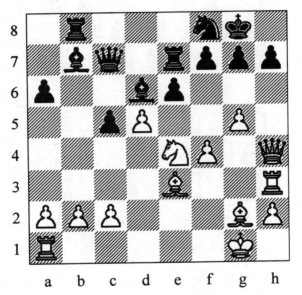

Once again my attack seems to be at a standstill, thanks to his excellent defensive knight on f8. The time has come, though, to deliver a crushing blow. What did I play?

1.Nf6 +! and the game is over. He played **1 . . . gxf6**, after which **2.gxf6 Bxd5 3.Qh6** forces mate on g7. I sacrificed a piece to open up the g-file and get rid of Black's defense. A very logical idea. Go back to the position after 1.Nf6. Black could have played 1 . . . Kh8. (See Diagram 40.)

40

WHITE TO MOVE:

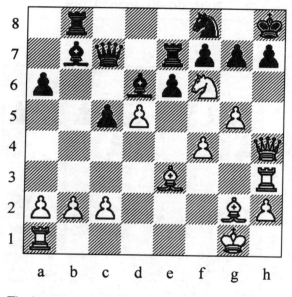

Find mate in two.

That's right, 2.Qxh7+!! a queen sacrifice to expose the black king. 2 . . . Nxh7 and 3.Rxh7 is mate.

We can see from the examples in this chapter how crucial the theme of busting open the position is in an attack. It is virtually impossible to checkmate a king that is well defended. The trick is to do away with the defense and then reap the benefits of abandoned royalty.

8 PAWN STORMS AND THE POWER OF THE KAMIKAZE

The pawn, as a rule, is the least valuable chess piece. For this reason the exchange of a pawn, or even two, for any other piece is hugely advantageous. All pieces must run from an attacking pawn, and conversely a pawn can be sacrificed to smash the defense if the chances for success look promising. The *pawn storm* is the rush of a phalanx of pawns at the enemy camp. This can include a mere pair of pawns or sometimes three or even four. It is not likely that you will be able to synchronize more than four pawns in a single attack. Let's see the position below.

I reached this position in a strong open tournament in Philadelphia when I was ten years old. White is clearly better, as I have an extra pawn and Black's pieces are in disarray. My bishops are bearing down on his kingside. In fact my position is winning, as I can destroy the black camp with an overwhelming pawn storm.

41 Waitzkin–Moore

NATIONAL CHESS CONGRESS UNDER-2000, 1987

WHITE TO MOVE:

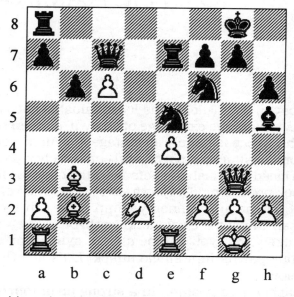

How should I initiate a pawn storm?

HINT: Note that a queen trade would be favorable to Black in this position. A very important rule of middlegame play in chess is that *if your opponent has the initiative or a special advantage (controls most of the board) and you are defending or lack breathing room, trade pieces.* This makes sense, as you are cutting down on the attackers or relieving some of the cramp in your position. Obviously the reverse applies if you have the initiative or a positional advantage. This is a chessic "law" that should not be followed blindly because in chess there are exceptions to every rule.

I mention this because in the above position the

queens are lined up to be traded if the black knight moves. The variation 1.Nc4 Nxc4 2.Bxf6 does not work because of 2 . . . Qxg3!, an *in-between move*; 3.hxg3 gxf6, and Black has not lost any material.

Correct is **1.f4!** Black is forced to play **1 . . . Ng6** because if he tries 1 . . . Nxc6, 2.Bxf6 wins as the g7-pawn is pinned, and if Black continues 1 . . . Neg4, White can trap the knight with 2.h3! After 1 . . . Ng6 I continued with the pawn storm: **2.e5!** Notice once again in Diagram 42 that the attempt 2.Bxf6 gxf6 3.f5 does not win the knight. Why?

42

BLACK TO MOVE:

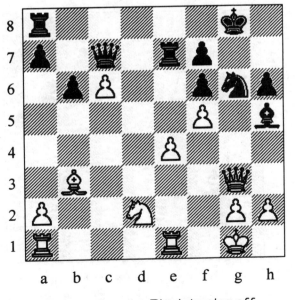

An in-between move. Black trades off pieces to deflate White's attack.

Because of 3 . . . Qxg3! removing the pinner and rescuing the knight.

After 2.e5, the black knights are forced to retreat further with **2 . . . Nh7**. Now take a few minutes to look at this position. Without calculating a move, you should be able to see that Black is in terrible shape. There is no coordination between his three minor pieces on the kingside, which are misplaced and cramped together, bullied by White's pawns. Their attacking potential is close to zero. They are just trying to survive. From a glance, a chess player should be able to tell that White has an overwhelming positional advantage.

43

WHITE TO MOVE:

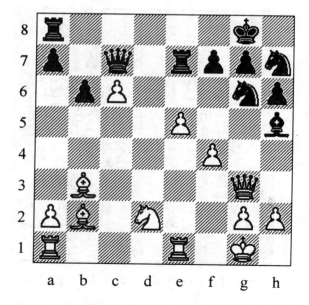

But once again, the realization of an advantage in chess depends upon technique and imagination. How should White continue?

Continue the pawn storm with **3.f5!** Black is being driven off the board. **3 . . . Nf8**.

Now let's find the crunching move for White. What is best? It is thematically consistent with the rest of the attack.

4.f6! The final blow, threatening mate on g7 and the rook on e7. Black finally got rid of the queens, but not until giving up a piece: **4 . . . Nxf6 5.exf6 Qxg3 6.hxg3**, and I went on to win easily.

This brings up another and in fact the most crucial point about exchanging pieces. When you are ahead in material it is almost always good to trade off the pieces. The endgame is the best place to take advantage of material superiority, as an extra piece or pawn is much more glaring. Let's consider the analogy of pieces of cake. If you have six pieces of a terrific chocolate cake and your friend has seven, it is no big deal because you both have lots of cake and one extra piece doesn't really matter. If you both pig out and eat five pieces each, now your friend has two pieces and you have one . . . here is something to be upset about.

In more mathematical terms, material inequality can be more easily exploited when the ratio of forces is broadened, which can be done by simply trading down. So in the above example I didn't let my opponent trade pieces until the scenario on the board made the exchange favorable for me.

The reader can see how a few aggressive pawn moves turned a better position into a winning one. Because a pawn has such a small value, it instills fear in everyone it meets. It has the power of the kamikaze!

9 QUEEN TRAPS

The queen is the most powerful and mobile piece on the chessboard. To capture her for little or no compensation is a great feat and almost always spells the end of the game. Because the queen can roam great distances quickly and moves like a rook and bishop combined, the idea of trapping her seems highly improbable; however, the very power and mobility of the queen can lead to her downfall. The player is lulled into a sense of the queen's immortality and doesn't take heed of subtle booby traps in her path; he guides her into enemy territory, lured by the opportunity to grab material. To trap a queen is a delicate art; nonetheless, it happens frequently in chess. More often than not it is the barrier of her own pawns combined with subtle tactics that cause the lady's downfall. The queen trap is usually quite shocking for the victim.

This game was played in the final round of the National High School Championships in 1992. I was in big time pressure and had three moves to make before time control. A few moves earlier I had come up with a fascinating idea that my opponent stumbled right into.

44 Raptis–Waitzkin
1992 NATIONAL HIGH SCHOOL CHAMPIONSHIPS

BLACK TO MOVE:

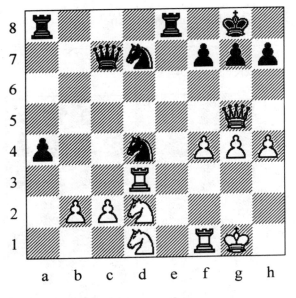

How can I trap his queen?

HINT: Remember the whole board!

I played **1 . . . Ra5!!**, which completely stunned him. The queen is gone. He played **2.f5**. What did I have planned now?

2 . . . h6! and he resigned. If 3.Qh5, then Nf6 wins the lady, and 3.Qf4 is met by Ne2+, a royal fork. Notice how the white pawns helped hem in their own queen. It is essential to be a street-smart chess player; understand your surroundings, the good and bad, and sometimes use the placement of opposing pieces for your own ends.

The next position involves a different kind of trap. My opponent, a strong master, is trying to develop an attack against my Sicilian Defense. His queen is wedged into my camp and he plans Rg1-g3-h3 and Qxh7 mate:

45   Mercuri—Waitzkin
NEW ENGLAND OPEN, 1989

BLACK TO MOVE:

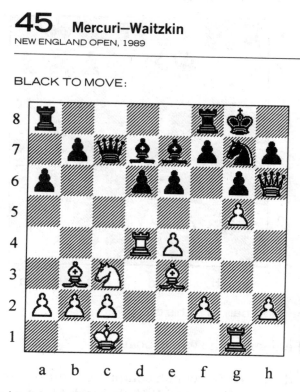

I came up with a trap a few moves earlier and in this position I put it into effect. What did I play?

1 . . . Nh5!! The queen has nowhere to go. I locked her inside my castle and will quickly close in for the kill. **2.e5 Rf-d8 3.Rh4 Bf8!** and the lady is no more. This was a different kind of trap, as I first rendered the queen immobile and only then did I worry about actually attacking her.

Here is a position from a game played in the fourth round of the 1989 National Elementary Championships.

46 Gottfried–Waitzkin
1989 NATIONAL ELEMENTARY CHAMPIONSHIPS

BLACK TO PLAY:

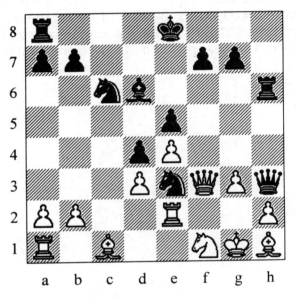

I have been attacking and cap it off with a nice queen trap. What is it?

1 . . . Rf6! and after **2.Bg2 Qh7** the queen has nowhere to run.

There are some types of positions that are wise to avoid for fear of getting your queen trapped. Often if there is a pawn or even a rook hanging deeply within the enemy camp, there is a trap waiting for your errant queen. Always think twice before placing royalty deep behind the enemy lines (recall the example against Mercuri). Ask yourself if the walls can close so she cannot get out. You must remember at the same time to trust yourself. If you have a tempting move and you don't see the problem with it, you must play it. *Never let fear govern your play!*

On the more positive side, keep an eye out for ways of snaring the enemy queen. Sometimes you can defend a pawn indirectly with the idea of luring the queen too far from home. This is the most common way of trapping the queen. The next position is a perfect example.

47

WHITE TO PLAY:

Has Black won a pawn?

Black just played Qb6+ and thinks himself very clever because he is forking the white king and the pawn on b2. At this point White smacks himself on the forehead and morosely shakes his head. He resignedly plays **1.Be3**, after which Black whips the pawn right off with **1 . . . Qxb2** and storms away from the board feeling like the king himself. (See Diagram 48.)

48

WHITE TO MOVE:

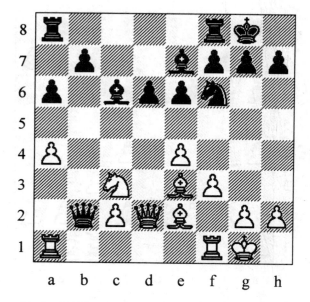

Ah, but White had laid a trap in this position and, with the help of a little body English, lured his opponent a bit too far. What did he have in mind?

2.Rfb1! and the black queen is finished. The a-rook takes away the a3 square, the b-rook attacks the queen and denies retreat along the file, and the Nc3, c2-pawn, and Qd2 combine to prevent any escape towards the kingside. The lady is a goner!

My final example of a queen trap is perhaps the most interesting. In chess, sometimes conceptions are rendered all the more fascinating because of off-the-board dramas that spectators know little or nothing about. Such was the case in the following game.

Rivalries develop over the years in any competitive environment, between players, players and coaches, teams, players and teams, and so on. I was a member of the Dalton School chess team and for many years, with the help of my best friend Dave Arnett, a terrific player, and four or five other talented kids, we won seven scholastic team championships. I should add that in the primary, elementary, junior high school, and senior high school national championships, which are sponsored by the United States Chess Federation, there are individual prizes as well as team awards. From the third grade until my freshman year in high school, when I retired from these scholastic events, I won five individual national titles while at the same time helping my team. In elementary school we were ably coached by Svetozar Jovanovic, and later on by my teacher and dear friend Bruce Pandolfini.

Every year that I participated, our arch-rival was the Hunter College Elementary School in New York City. Before the Dalton glory days Hunter won at the Nationals nearly every year. But during my years at Dalton we had a great team and managed to edge out Hunter year after year. Each spring the Hunter coach, Sunil Weeramantry, a superb chess teacher and author, came to the Nationals stocked with strategies to beat Dalton, and with dangerous opening variations to defeat Waitzkin. It seemed as though Sunil plotted and planned all year for this great show in the spring when over a thousand chess-crazy kids would show up in Charlotte, Salt Lake City, Atlanta, Detroit, or wherever, to compete for the big trophies. Bruce Pandolfini used to call Sunil Weeramantry "the Wizard," because of all the coaches, Sunil was the best prepared, the cleverest motivator, and a miracle worker at squeezing out great team results at these wonderful events—results that were perhaps even better than the sum of his players.

Sunil was always entertaining to watch during these events, wringing his hands when one of his players hung a piece or offered a draw with the better position. I would see him striding through the lobby ecstatically when one of his players had pulled off an upset. But years of close losses surely took a toll on the Wizard. At the closing ceremony when the purple-shirted Hunter team lined up for second place honors, Sunil looked like despair itself, washed out and gray from exhaustion and defeat. Nonetheless, each spring he came back with renewed energy and dedication to annihilate Dalton and crush Waitzkin.

For several years first board on the Hunter team was Michael Granne, a clever tactician. Sunil prepared him well for our games, but Michael never beat me in the Nationals, nor did any other Hunter player that I can recall. In the following game against Granne you will notice that I am saddled with what appears to be a losing position.

I would urge the beginner to play the moves out on a board. As will sometimes be the case in the later chapters of this book, do not be frustrated if you cannot visualize all of this in your head. Appreciate the flow of the tactics and the ideas. I assure you that the ability to visualize long variations will improve with practice and more practice.

I am about to drop my rook to Michael's knight. I will never forget the sight of the Wizard when he saw my quandary, his mouth pursed, eyelids twitching a little, a smile spreading across his face. I was told later that when he walked away from the board he clenched his hands and said again and again, "We've got him, we've got him." Well . . . almost, Sunil, almost.

49 Granne—Waitzkin

1989 NATIONAL JUNIOR HIGH SCHOOL CHAMPIONSHIPS

BLACK TO MOVE:

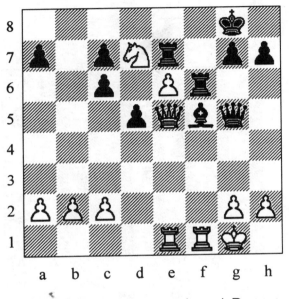

Set this position up on your board. Do you
see any possibilities for me?

Everyone thought I was losing, as my rook is attacked
and cannot stay on the crucial f-file. If for instance I play
1 . . . Rg6, threatening mate in one, White replies 2.g3!
and next will take the bishop on f5, and if the f5-bishop
moves, Rf8 is mate.

However, I had done a long calculation the move before and discovered a variation where I would sac my
queen, eventually winning back my deficit in material by
setting a subtle trap on Mike's queen. In fact the queen
will not be lost but is so dominated by my rooks that she
must give up the knight to survive.

1 . . . Rfxe6 2.Rxf5! Qxf5!! (if I had played 2 . . . Rxe5, what would White play? 3.Rf8 mate!) **3.Qxf5 Rxe1+ 4.Kf2 R1e2+ 5.Kg3 R2e3+ 6.Kh4.**

50

BLACK TO MOVE:

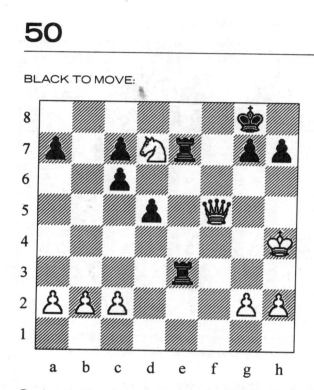

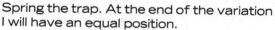

Spring the trap. At the end of the variation I will have an equal position.

6 . . . Rf7! and I win a knight, thanks to his near-gone queen. After **7.Nf6+ Rxf6 8.Qc8+** the game was soon drawn.

What did I have planned against 7.Qg4, which both escapes the rook attack and defends the knight?

51

BLACK TO MOVE:

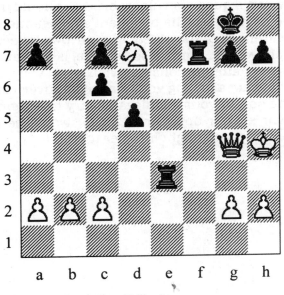

The position after 7.Qg4.

The skewer 7 . . . Re4! wins the queen.

7.Qg5 would be met by 7 . . . Re4+ to protect the rook, followed by 8 . . . Rxd7, and after 7.Qh5 simply 7 . . . Rxd7. There is no way to protect the knight. Notice how the rooks take away virtually all of the queen's escape squares. I had to see that all of these complications were okay for me before I allowed the original diagrammed position. You can see how important it is to work on calculation and visualization of the chessboard. To this end it is a useful exercise to try to play blindfold games. At first you will not see anything, but then the board will start to be visible and you will be able to remember the position for a few moves. Someday, with work, you might even be able to play a whole game without looking at the board!

I hope you have some sense, after studying this chapter, of when a queen is vulnerable. You should use these ideas to help snatch the opponent's queen and to maintain awareness of the safety of your own queen. Again and again we find that chess, like life, is a balancing act: you must maintain constant vigil over your precious lady, while not allowing your play to be governed by fear of losing her. In your middlegames try to imagine situations where your opponent's queen would be in peril, and then how you might lure her there.

10 MINOR TRAPS

It is much more often that a minor piece will be trapped rather than a queen. This makes sense, as knights and bishops are considerably less mobile and cannot escape so easily as Her Majesty. As a rule, pieces can be trapped much more readily on the side of the board because their mobility is limited. Consider the position below.

52

WHITE TO MOVE:

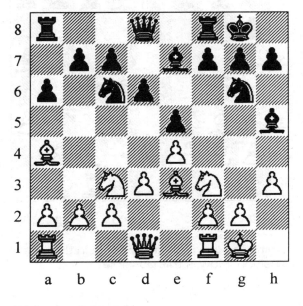

White can win a piece.

White can win a piece with **1.g4!**. The bishop is so confined by the edge of the board and its own knight that there is nowhere to run. This kingside expansion is, in fact, a typical device to break a pin like the one on my knight on f3. Usually the bishop can retreat to g6, but the black knight in the diagram is badly misplaced. Sometimes a piece trap can be connived even when g6 is vacant:

53

WHITE TO MOVE:

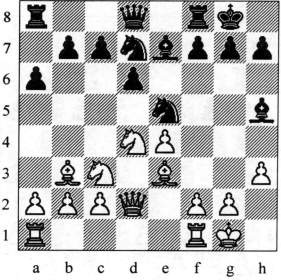

White can win a piece by force in this position. How is this possible?

By advancing the kingside pawn phalanx White can overwhelm the black bishop. The first move is **1.f4!** attacking the black knight. He must retreat with **1 . . . Nc6**. Now we go after the bishop with **2.g4!** Black must run with **2 . . . Bg6**, and after **3.f5!** the poor fellow is smothered and must be lost.

54

BLACK'S BISHOP IS LOST:

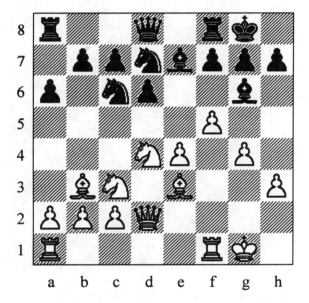

Keep in mind that advancing the kingside pawns should always be done cautiously. You do not want to recklessly throw the cover away from your king, as this can backfire. If your own attack is not rapid and decisive you may find yourself on the receiving end of checkmate.

There is a peculiar relationship that exists between bishops and knights. The knight is the only piece that can jump over others and has a strange, evasive pattern of movement, but when located at the side of the board, it can be completely dominated by a bishop:

55

WHITE TO MOVE:

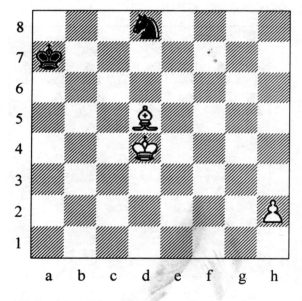

White wins this position easily. How?

The knight cannot move anywhere without being taken. This is called a **"corral."** White wins by simply pushing the h-pawn all the way up the board. The black knight is helpless to defend.

The above relationship, two squares vertically or horizontally between bishop and knight on the side of the board, is often a decisive setup in endgames when another piece can march over and pick the ripe fruit. Take, for example, the following position:

56

WHITE TO MOVE:

What is White's best move?

HINT: White wins by corralling the knight and then marching over to capture.

Best is **1.Bd4!** and the knight cannot move. The game could continue 1 . . . Kg6 2.Kd2 Kf7 3.Kc2 Ke6 4.Kb3 Kd5 5.Kxa4, and White will easily pick up the black pawns, make a queen, and win the game. The black king was unable to assist his piece in time. In fact he missed by only one move, as the black king on d5 defends the c5 escape square and the knight would have leaped out of the trap next move.

One more way to trap a piece is to use a device that I examined in the last chapter on queen traps. We can lure an enemy warrior too far from home and then lock it into our part of the board. This is what I did to Lou Mercuri's queen, if you recall. More often this is a way to snare bishops. Here is an example:

57

WHITE TO MOVE:

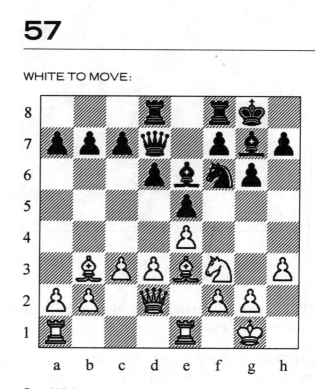

Can White pick up a pawn?

It is White's move and a pawn is hanging on a7. At first glance this seems like a fruit ripe for picking, but your sense of danger should kick into action right about now. In fact, to play **1.Bxa7** is one of the oldest mistakes in the book! How can Black trap the bishop?

58

BLACK TO MOVE:

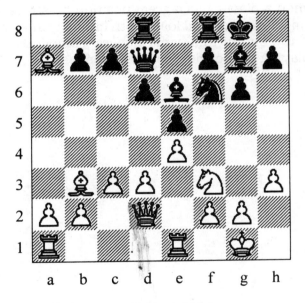

Just a simple move. Lock him in.

1 . . . b6! and the fella is never going to get out. Black will, at his leisure, play Rd8-a8 and capture the trapped piece. It is very dangerous to send one of your soldiers on a solo trip behind enemy lines. Be aware of the peril.

In the next example, from one of my recent games, we see how a knight that wandered too far from the center and into enemy territory found itself trapped. My opponent was National Master Norman "Pete" Rogers. Before we get to the key position it is worth mentioning that for much of this game I had been defending a very poor position. After Rogers played several inaccurate moves we arrived at an endgame that was roughly equal. The proper result at this point would have been to agree to a draw. But, after playing most of the game from a superior position, this was hard for Rogers to accept. Often when a player has a great position he starts to take the win for granted and loses both intensity and objectivity. At the end of this game Rogers' competitive desire was playing havoc with his chess sense.

59 Rogers—Waitzkin

MURPHY AFC INTERNATIONAL, 1994

BLACK TO MOVE:

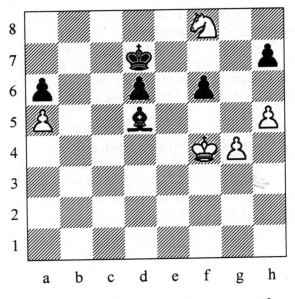

My opponent didn't sense the danger of the position.

In this position Pete believed that he was winning. His plan was to take my h-pawn and then win the game with his outside passed pawn. But I had seen that Nf8 would be a big mistake. Rogers is an excellent tactician and chances are that he erred because he was still in the "winning mood" and didn't have a sense for the danger of the position. Using the principles that we have studied above, find my next two moves to win his knight.

I played **1 . . . Ke7 2.Nxh7 Bg8!** and there is no-where to run. Once again, the side of the board spells the fall of a wandering knight.

Now we understand the vulnerability of pieces on the edge of the board—the board itself has the piece half-trapped. My first coach, Bruce Pandolfini, used to tell me, "A knight on the rim is very grim." This is completely true. Speaking in mathematical terms alone, a knight on the "rim" can jump to only four squares while a central-ized knight hits eight. Remember this at all times. The center is the most important part of the board and so in many cases you should try to place your pieces there.

Having understood this essential law of centralized pieces, let's see an exception. I reached the next position against Daniels Fridmans, the Latvian representative in the 1992 World Under-16 Championship in Duisburg, Germany. I felt that my position was okay and had no idea what was about to happen to me.

60 Fridmans–Waitzkin

1992 WORLD UNDER-16 CHAMPIONSHIP

WHITE TO MOVE:

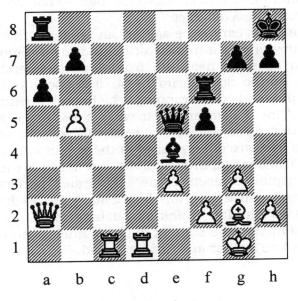

White can win my bishop in one move.

He played **1.f3!** and I am in big trouble, as my bishop is trapped! With my piece in the middle of the board I had no sense of danger. One of many cruel little lessons in a chess career. You must always be aware of all possibilities. Not much can be taken for granted in a chess game.

In fact, bishops, queens, and rooks are distance operators and frequently control the center from afar. A rook sitting on e4 in a complex middlegame is often more a target than anything else. In the above position the bishop paid dearly for its central location. The key is to control the center, not necessarily to occupy it. A player must use his judgement. Ultimately one gains a feel for centralization through the interplay of chess axioms and experience. There are times when queens and bishops are well placed in the center and other times when it is safer and more effective for them to control central squares from a distance.

The same cannot be said about knights! These guys specialize in close maneuvering and for the most part should be used near the front lines. Remember, "A knight on the rim is grim!" Also, it is useful to keep in mind the method of trapping a bishop by a wing pawn storm. This is a clever way to win a chess game. Keep in mind that piece traps are a relatively indirect weapon, and so they are often missed at the end of long calculations. The Michael Granne game, discussed in the previous chapter, "Queen Traps," illustrates perfectly the need to visualize the entire board many moves down the line. A weightlifter trains by pushing more and more iron; similarly, the student of chess must push himself to calculate further and further ahead.

11 COURAGE

There comes a moment in many attacks when a player has to shed all supports and make the final dash, the decisive thrust, while leaving his or her own king to the elements, so to speak. When a chess game comes down to a race for the king, both sides attacking aggressively, it is not only a question of who can do the most accurate calculation, although this is crucial. *At the critical moment victory often comes to the player who trusts his calculation, and more, who heeds his intuition when the position is impossible to calculate fully.* This is a time when a player must have faith. Often the critical move or moves entail leaving the king to fend for himself while believing that he will survive long enough for you to get the enemy's king first. More often, though, the dramatic conclusion is not a simple "High Noon" shoot-out. Sometimes victory will hang on the player's icy assessment of the value of grabbing material relative to the threat of allowing his opponent attacking initiative. Consider the following position.

61 Waitzkin–Sabri Abdul
1992 WORLD UNDER-16 CHAMPIONSHIPS

WHITE TO MOVE:

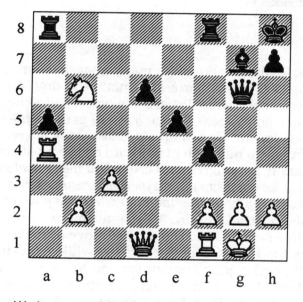

We have reached a critical moment in the game.

After making a long calculation, my opponent's last move was . . . f4. He has sacrificed a rook, daring me to take it. His conclusion was that if I took the material, he would mate me. I am forced to make a decision. I can take the rook, understanding that he will play 1 . . . f3 and after 2.g3, try to wedge his queen into h3 and play Qg2 mate. Or I can simply play 1.f3, stop his attack, and go about my business. The white position would certainly be better then because of his weak a-pawn and my strong knight vs. his weak bishop. (The bishop is bad because all of his central pawns are on the same color, blocking him in.) To play 1.Nxa8 I must calculate that in all lines I am not being mated. This is a hard task, but on the other hand, if I am successful I will win easily, being up the exchange.

Try to calculate the implications and decide whether I should play 1.Nxa8 or 1.f3.

After a long calculation I decided that I could defend mate in every variation and played **1.Nxa8!** To make a decision like this a player must have full confidence in his/her calculating ability. It all came down to who saw more. It turns out that I did. Let's see what the difference was.

He played **1 . . . f3** as expected. I must play **2.g3** or else Qxg2 will be mate. My opponent played **2 . . . Qe6**, threatening Qh3 and Qg2 as I mentioned above. What should I play now?

62

WHITE TO MOVE:

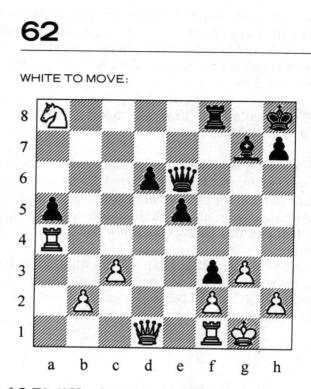

I played **3.Rh4!** He played **3 . . . Bf6**. It is in this position that I had seen more than my opponent. What should I play now?

63

WHITE TO MOVE:

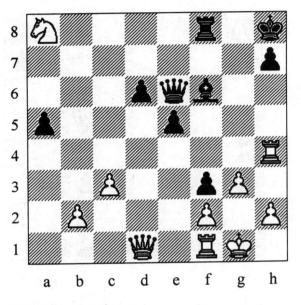

Stop the attack.

4.Qxf3! and the bishop can't take on h4 because of the pin to the Rf8. He retreated with **4 . . . Qg8**, after which the attack was over and I went on to win easily.

Let's go back to the position where he played 2 . . . Qe6 and consider 2 . . . Qf5 instead. (See Diagram 64.)

64

WHITE TO MOVE:

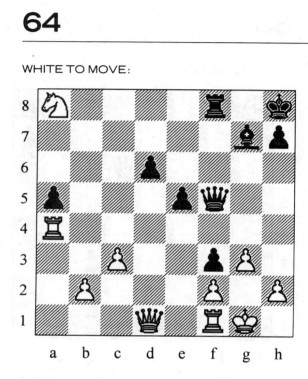

Is there a difference? Now after 3.Rh4
Bf6! would be very strong as the rook is in
trouble and there is no 4.Qxf3. What can I
play after 2 . . . Qf5?

I was going to respond with 3.g4! Qf6 4.Kh1 followed by
Rg1, winning because his attack is stopped and I can
convert my material advantage.

Now wait just a minute. Take what I just said and look
back at the position after 2 . . . Qe6.

65

WHITE TO MOVE:

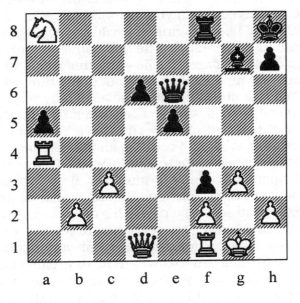

Is there another defense?

Of course! 3.Kh1 Qh3 4.Rg1 stops mate and will be very strong. If 4 . . . Rf6, then 5.Rh4 stops the attack cold.

When my opponent made the rook sacrifice to craft a mating attack, I decided he had made a terrible mistake. A player must have complete confidence in his or her calculation and judgement. Never assume your opponent sees more than you do. To the contrary, work harder than your opponent and see more. If you suspect your opponent has a trap waiting, find the trap. If you don't see it, then play what looks best to you. In the above position my opponent believed that he had set a winning trap. I proved to myself that he was wrong and took the rook. It was a good chess fight.

Recently, after one of my games in a youth world championship, my opponent said to me, "I had decided before we played that if you sacrificed a piece, I wouldn't take it." I had been playing in a wild and aggressive style throughout the event and he had come up with a game plan to duck my dares. To be sure, this was a nice compliment, but my opponent was not doing himself any favors. When a chess player is governed by fear there is no hope of being first-rate. I can think of numerous examples of talented players who have been impeded in their careers by lack of courage and fearfulness.

One of my peers, for example, would frequently drop out of open tournaments after the first two or three rounds when it was obvious that he would be paired in the next round against a player his own strength or even stronger. In this way, for years he nursed his rating in a rather risk-free fashion. This boy was very talented and I am sure he believed that when the time came he would be able to compete favorably against other top players—he was just putting off the day. Then there came a time when he was invited to play in a "closed" or round robin event where everyone was at least as good as he was. Predictably, after losing two early games, he withdrew claiming sickness, which threw the tournament into chaos. In retrospect this was a foreseeable result. He had pandered to his fears for years and had no resources to draw upon when he finally found himself in a pressured situation.

Another boy was very good at playing openings but as soon as the position became double-edged, with both sides attacking the king, he would retreat his attackers and construct a little fortress for his king. Fear made this boy play like an ostrich. Nonetheless, he was sometimes able to draw games against good players with his fortresses. For his age this boy was a good technical player and frequently he won his games against juniors and weaker players.

In one scholastic national championship this boy played very well and found himself in the last round competing for first place. I urged him to play at all costs for the win. "Second place is not an option," I told him, as he has always been a player who falls just short of the big win. "Don't offer any draws even if your position is worse." He nodded but I suspected that he would have difficulty in this high-pressure game. For years he had cultivated the habit of trying to draw big games instead of taking a risk to try to win. If he was ever going to become a good player he would have to break through this psychological barrier.

As it turned out in the game, his opening preparation was right on target and the boy quickly achieved a superior position. In the middlegame he built a winning attack and everything pointed to a national championship. Then from across the room I could see the two of them shaking hands. Our player must have won, a few friends commented, but I had my suspicions. Sure enough, our player had offered his opponent a draw. This other guy must have been stunned. The position on the board at the moment of the draw offer was completely winning for our player. He was only two or three moves away from the national championship but he was too blinded by his fear to play them.

Fear, of course, is not an easy opponent to beat. World champion Garry Kasparov says that when he feels *fear* or *lack of confidence* (all chessplayers feel this way from time to time), he *pretends to be confident*. He tries to play the moves he would play if he were feeling confident. Maybe this is the best advice.

In the next example, a combination of calculation and confidence is once again the key.

66   Waitzkin–Steinhoff
WORLD UNDER-16 CHAMPIONSHIPS, 1992

WHITE TO MOVE:

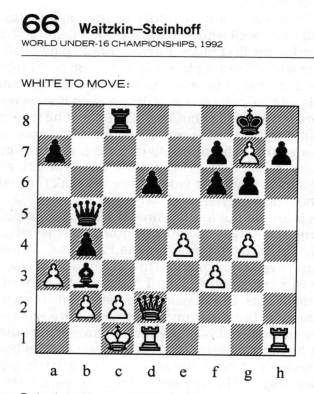

Calculate the variations and remember,
have courage!

I played **1.Qh6!** abandoning my king even though Black had a lot of firepower coming at me. But I had my own attacking ideas. Now I will mate Black next move with Qxh7, so he must keep on checking me. I had to calculate a lot of complications to play this one. The question is simple: can I get out of checks? Let's investigate some of the lines that I saw: **1 . . . Rxc2+ 2.Kb1 Rxb2**—this is the only chance for Black, as any non-check is tragic. I must play **3.Kxb2**.

67

BLACK TO MOVE:

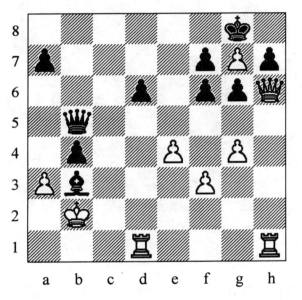

Black must check or die!

It is in this position that my analysis must begin. My opponent has two possible continuations. He played **3 . . . Qe5+**, and the alternative was 3 . . . bxa3+. Now the reader should make a decision. I am going to give all of the lines that I calculated during the game to justify playing 1.Qh6. The more advanced students should try to follow the lines, but if you are not so confident just stick to the main continuation.

Let's look at 3 . . . bxa3+ first. (See Diagram 68.)

68

WHITE TO MOVE:

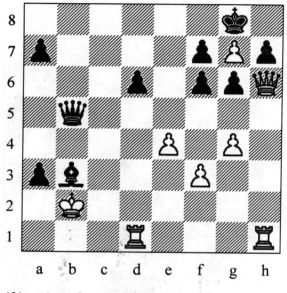

If he plays 3 . . . bxa3 + ...

How do you think I should continue? There are two legit-
imate responses: 4.Kxa3 and 4.Kc3. One of these moves
wins and one doesn't. If you are interested in tackling a
tough exercise, sit down with a board and try to figure
out which move is correct. If you can't calculate the variations, then play them out on your board.

First let's consider 4.Kxa3. Black must always check,
so: 4 . . . Qa4+ 5.Kb2 Qa2+ 6.Kc3 Qc2+ 7.Kd4 Qf2+ 8.Qe3
Qb2+ 9.Qc3 Qf2+ 10.Qe3 Qb2+ 11.Qc3 Qf2+ 12.Kd3 if I
want to play for a win. If not I can just keep on repeating
to draw. 12 . . . Qxf3+ 13.Kd2 Bxd1! 14.Rxd1 Qf4+ 15.Qe3
Qxg4 16.Qh6 Qxe4.

69

WHITE TO MOVE:

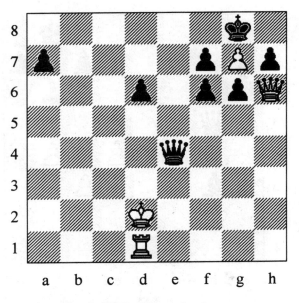

After 4.Kxa3, White cannot win.

White cannot win because my king is too exposed and Black has too many pawns for my rook. The black king is impossible to attack because mine has no shelter. This is a very difficult conclusion to reach, especially after such a long calculation (I am up a rook after all). It is comforting, at least, that I can have a draw if I want it. This is a useful device in the calculation of complex positions. Having a "fall-back variation," in addition to being a very practical option, can give you added confidence in your assessments of a wild position.

Let's go back now to the position after Black's third move. (See Diagram 70.)

70

WHITE TO MOVE:

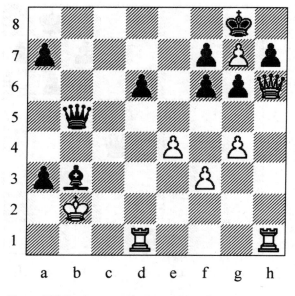

Does White have other options?

We see that 4.Kxa3 does not work so well. Best is 4.Kc3!
and after 4 . . . Qc4+ (Black must protect his bishop)
5.Kd2 Qd4+ (5 . . . Qc2+ 6.Ke3 Qc5+ 7.Rd4 Qc3+ 8.Rd3
Qc5+ 9.Ke2 Qc2+ 10.Qd2 Qxd2+ 11.Kxd2 wins) 6.Ke2
Bc4+ 7.Ke1 Qc3+ 8.Kf2 Qc2+ 9.Kg3. If you skipped over
this calculation because it was too long, then take a deep
breath and go back and play it out on your board. This is
what makes a good chess player.

71

MY KING ESCAPES:

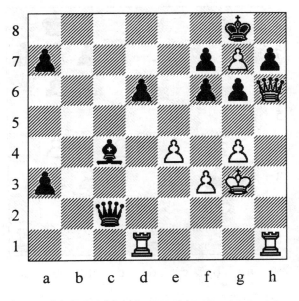

I am winning without a problem.

So all of these lines handle 3 . . . bxa3, which is just one of my opponent's possibilities. It turns out that this was the move that I was most concerned with because I had found the refutation to 3 . . . Qe5+ quickly. He did, indeed, play **3 . . . Qe5+**. How should I respond?

72

WHITE TO MOVE:

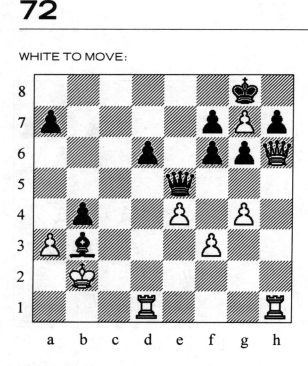

In this position you need to calculate more than one line.

Again there are two main possibilities: 4.Kxb3 and 4.Kb1. A poor alternative, 4.Kc1 gets mated after . . . Qc3+, and 4.Kxb3 is a mistake because of 4 . . . Qc3+ 5.Ka4 Qc2+ 6.Kxb4:

73

BLACK TO MOVE:

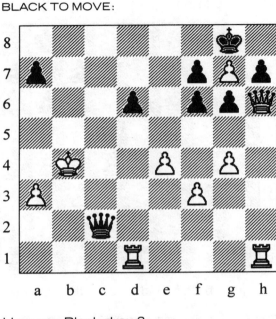

How can Black draw?

Black responds with 6 . . . a5 + ! 7.Kxa5 Qc5 + 8.Ka6 Qc6 +, and Black has perpetual check.

So, after 3 . . . Qe5 +, this leaves only **4.Kb1**, which I played and had seen when I played 1.Qh6. (See Diagram 74.)

74

WHITE TO MOVE:

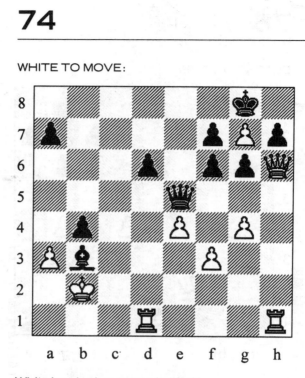

White's winning move is Kb1!

The game finished **4 . . . Bc2+ 5.Kc1! Qa1+ 6.Kd2 Qd4+ 7.Ke2** and Black resigned because he will soon run out of checks. My king will find shelter behind my kingside pawns, and I will be up a rook.

So these were a lot of lines to calculate, huh? In fact I did see almost all of the lines above when I played 1.Qh6, but not all! It is impossible to see all possibilities in a chess game even if you are a fantastic tactician. The secret is to know how to approach such a problem. Finding the correct move in a complex chess position is no accident. It is often not from brute-force calculation that we reach the correct conclusion. There is an entire thought process that one develops from training and tournament experience. One very useful method is to identify *move candidates*.

In a given position the player should, before going into deep calculation, note the three or four moves that seem most reasonable. This way you will not miss something silly. After you have your three or four possible lines, you start to analyze. The moves that seem more dubious should be dealt with and discarded first. Often the correct move can be reached by a simple process of elimination.

If you go back to the original diagrammed position you might notice that I do not have so many alternatives to consider. In fact, my move is just about forced unless I am willing to make a material concession. I had actually planned 1.Qh6 a few moves before the first diagram! I had then seen 4.Kb1 and had calculated all the variations far enough to see *that I could not lose and that I probably could win.* If you recall the one variation in which he ended up with perpetual check and the one in which he had many pawns for my rook, I was never worse. This was like having a little insurance policy. One must learn to be a pragmatic thinker. I saw enough lines to be comfortable with my decision, went for it, and was rewarded.

Self-confidence was perhaps my biggest asset in this game. Garry Kasparov once said that feeling confident was almost like holding a material advantage. I can firmly vouch for this, as there have been times in my chess career when for one reason or another I lacked belief in myself. Playing games in this condition is a terrible uphill battle, but from time to time it happens to everyone: your assessment of positions is shaky, every move your opponent makes is filled with dire threats, you feel afraid of your shadow. What to do?

The use of "fall-back variations" is an excellent device with very practical significance. I can recall a number of games in which I was forced to play a line that I had noted as a safety after realizing that there was a gaping hole in my analysis in my primary variation.

Top competitors often set up artificial devices to regain their balance. If your confidence is shot, find some way to gain it back during competition. Although self-manipulation goes against my grain, I have discovered that it is sometimes essential. NBA and NFL players work with sports psychologists to win back lost confidence. Little things help. Sit up straight in your chair. Look confident. Work on your game face. Try to recall how you felt when you were playing great chess one or two months before. Ask yourself what you would have played in the position if you were feeling confident. Remember, "You gotta believe!"

12 DON'T SETTLE FOR LESS

In a chess game you are constantly making decisions. In the beginning you are deciding where to develop your pieces, how to gain control of the center, how to begin an attack. Sometimes you are picking between the lesser of two evils, but more often, I hope, you are deciding which ripe fruit to grab. The chess game is an intense battle, and often when a fighter sees a glimmer of weakness, he will lunge for it instantly. However, there are times when it is better to hold back, to be patient and watch, or better yet, to pick at it a little, as the scratch rips into a gaping wound. "Maintain the tension," Gregory Kaidanov always reminds me. For the past two years Gregory has been my coach and has become one of my closest friends. He is unique in chess, a world-class grandmaster who loves to teach perhaps even more than to play. Gregory has a tremendous feel for the balance between action and patience in chess.

If you recall the chapter on discoveries, my game against Valente first brought up the idea of *maintaining the tension*. Gregory frequently reminds me to hold back on the tactics until they work out perfectly. In the Valente game I tried to improve my position until my discoveries worked, and only then did I open fire. Remember that your opponent is always plotting to get you, and when you are winning he is working harder than ever to find a way out. It is dangerous to play with a wounded animal. We must learn to be precise about the assessment of our advantage. Never settle for a pawn when you can soon win a rook. Why take an opponent's queen when you have forced mate? Let's look at the position below.

75 Waitzkin–McPartlan

1987 NEW YORK STATE CHAMPIONSHIP UNDER-2000

WHITE TO MOVE:

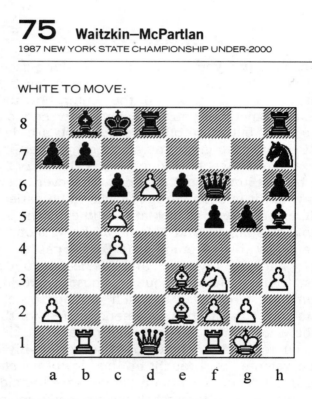

White's position is clearly better, as Black's bishop on b8 is hemmed in and his kingside is weak due to the open b-file. Also, I have a very strong move now. What did I play?

I skewered his queen to his rook with **1.Bd4!** to which he responded with **1 . . . Qf8.** And now the decisions begin. The natural impulse of the inexperienced player will be to win the exchange with 2.Bxh8. This would be an amateurish decision. After taking the rook White would be better but would still have a long struggle ahead. And during such a fight there are many ways to go wrong. Probably White would win, but maybe not.

76

WHITE TO MOVE:

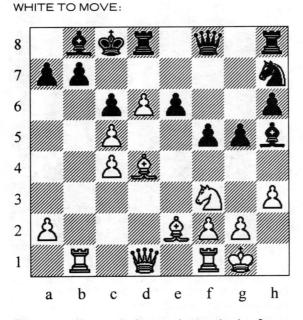

The experienced player always looks for the jugular. What is my best move here?

I threatened mate with **2.Qb3**. His rook on h8 isn't going anywhere and I completely dominate the board thanks to my bishop on d4. Even if in the strictest sense a rook is worth more than a bishop, who is doing more now? He defended the b7-pawn with **2 . . . Rd7**. How should I continue the attack?

77

WHITE TO MOVE:

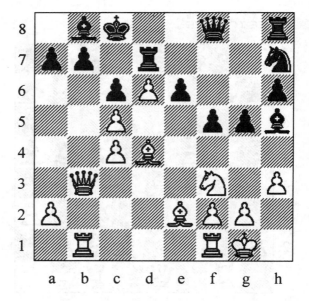

Now, I'm sure that once again a lot of readers want to take the rook, but *hold back, don't settle for less!*

3.Ne5! attacking the rook that defends mate and opening up a discovered attack on the Bh5. My opponent played **3 . . . Rg7**, getting away from my knight and still defending mate. Notice that if 3 . . . Bxe2, then after 4.Nxd7 Kxd7 5.Qxb7 Black's whole camp is falling. We have been patient so far. First we could have won the exchange, now his bishop is *en prise* on h5. After 4.Bxh5 I am up a piece and without question winning. But should I take the bishop? Is this my best move? Is there something stronger?

78

WHITE TO MOVE:

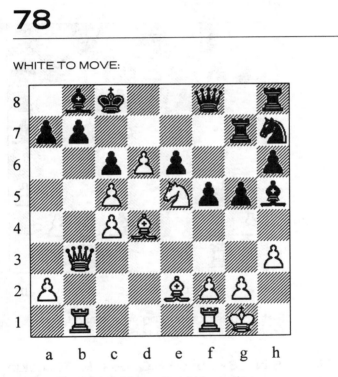

I went for more. How should I continue the attack?

HINT: Block the defense of b7.

I played **4.d7+!** cutting off Black's defense of the seventh rank. He played 4 . . . Kd8, as 4 . . . Rxd7 5.Nxd7 is tragic. How do you think White should continue the attack after **4 . . . Kd8**?

79

WHITE TO MOVE:

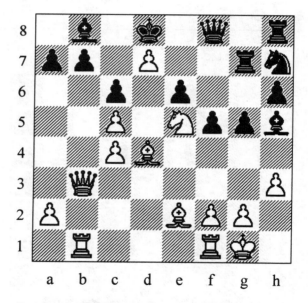

Set up this position on your board and study until you have found it.

I played **5.Nxc6+! bxc6 6.Qxb8+ Ke7**. Looking back, at first I could have won the exchange, later a bishop, and now his king is running, a rook is still hanging, the bishop on h5 is still hanging . . . am I going to take them? You've got to be kidding.

80

WHITE TO MOVE:

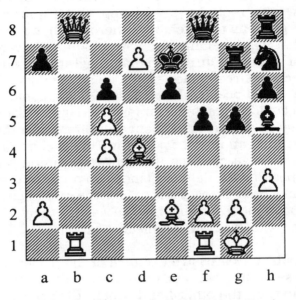

I've resisted this long; let's keep the attack rolling! What should I play?

HINT: Clear the lines for attack.

I prepared the entrance of my rook into the attack with **7.d8 (Q)+!** His response **7 . . . Qxd8** was forced and after **8.Rb7+** he resigned, as after 8 . . . Qd7, the only legal move, the black queen, rooks, and bishop are all under fire (8 . . . Ke8 gets squashed by 9.Bxh5+! and after 8 . . . Kf8 I simply take the hanging queen with 9.Qxd8+). Think about how far we have come. Initially, I was considering taking the exchange. In the end, I took the whole house. Do you see the power of going for the most you can get?

But let's look once more at the original position. There was still another element in my decision to refuse to take the rook for my bishop. Sometimes when a player gives up the exchange, there is a bug in his position that will be eliminated with only a relatively small loss of material. In the original diagram, to give away my dark-squared bishop would be a big mistake, as his queen would occupy the critical a1-h8 diagonal and my knight couldn't reach the fantastic e5 square. Sacrifice of material at the right moment will often ease the pressure against an inferior position. This is especially true with exchange sacs, as it is not uncommon that in a given position a knight or bishop can prove more powerful than a rook. By refusing to take the exchange I forced my opponent to cramp his pieces together. With my help, he was destroying himself.

This is a progressive example of the power of refusing to settle for less. But I must caution you that there are times, on the other hand, when it is correct to take what is given. In fact this is usually the case. Winning material is a great way to win a chess game. The win of a minor piece, or even a pawn, is usually enough to win with good technique. The best advice is to take the most that the position offers. As you become a more experienced player accurate assessments will become more natural. Sometimes not settling for less means being patient and prodding the position a little, and other times it means taking what you are given.

OPENING TRAPS

When a child begins his study of chess he is a tabula rasa, a clean slate. He has little or no understanding of where this study of chess will lead. Will he become an attacking player or a technical specialist who likes to grind out wins in the endgame? Will he spend all of his time studying openings, determined to gain a decisive advantage in the beginning of the game? The child doesn't care about these questions or even think about them. This new game is fun. The thrill of mobilizing the pieces, trying to win with exciting new strategies, drives him to learn, ideally with the guidance of a systematic and sensitive chess coach.

The early training of a player will largely mold his or her philosophy relative to the game. When I was a little boy, my teacher Bruce Pandolfini, in his soft manner (let's not confuse the real Bruce with the somewhat tyrannical character Ben Kingsley played in the movie *Searching for Bobby Fischer*), imposed his own thoughtful approach to the game. Many coaches of promising young students tend to focus on the openings. This is a very attractive idea because smart students easily memorize traps and win many games quickly.

Bruce had little patience for opening study. When I was seven and eight years old Bruce urged me to study the endgame and to hone my tactical skills. Opening novelties come and go, he would tell me, but the rules of the endgame never change. As a little boy I learned how to play chess, not how to make moves that I knew by heart. Sure enough, I would sometimes get lousy positions out of the opening, but almost invariably I would play myself out of trouble and win. The other kid might have learned some slick opening traps, but more often than not he didn't know what to do with a winning position once he achieved it.

In our five years working together Bruce rarely lost sight of the most important fundamental of all: the game had to be fun. Surely the greatest gift that he gave me was the example of his own love for chess. In his elegant manner he instilled in me a passion for chess that has never died. This should be the primary objective of a first coach; "you gotta have the love," as the saying goes. There are many examples of teachers whose students showed promise but then later quit chess. I believe this is largely due to the fact that the teachers were so involved with achieving instant success that they forgot about the child trying to have fun. If a coach has a vision of his student becoming a great player, it is very important not to be over-involved with immediate results. If the player has a solid understanding of chess, then the rest will come easily.

This understood, I was never a player entirely without opening knowledge. That would be silly. There are fundamentals to learn about opening play that should complement middlegame and endgame understanding. Bruce and I worked sparingly on the beginning of the game (in recent years I have had to study openings very deeply in order to develop as a strong master) but even as a beginner I had some ideas that I understood and played often. While a student should not overly stress the opening, particularly a beginner, it is necessary to be aware of various traps that you might fall into within the setups you normally play. There is nothing more depressing than to lose a big game before you even have a chance to plant your feet. It is also quite enjoyable to catch your opponent in a trap.

Included in this chapter are two of my games, decisive last-round contests with the national championship on the line. Each of them was decided by an opening trap. The first example I lost, the second I won.

The seventh round of the 1985 National Primary Championship was a crushing event in my young life. All that year I had been a terror, beating up on adults each afternoon in Washington Square Park. To me chess was winning. My rating was an unbeatable 1595. Going into the final round tied for first place, my confidence was high. Perhaps if I had known something about my opponent I would have been more on guard. David Arnett was a math genius in the second grade at The Dalton School, one of the first schools in the United States to incorporate chess into the curriculum. Since kindergarten, David had been well-taught at chess by the Dalton coach, Svetozar Jovanovic. But I knew nothing about either David or Dalton at the time. I was certain going into this game that I would win. I didn't lose to little kids. And this one looked nervous. His hand trembled when he made his moves. His rating was only 1441. But he beat me, crushed me. What a lesson that was!

This loss haunted me for years. It is incredible now when I think back on it. We were just two little kids, but we were playing for a national title. Such pressure! Untold glory for the champ, and so much remorse for the loser. I am not sure that little kids should have to go through this. Maybe the stakes are too high for eight- and nine-year-olds. My own father was so nervous that he never even came into the tournament hall. He waited outside beneath a tree, imagining our celebration after I won.

Although I was only eight years old, this one game changed me. For weeks afterwards I felt physically weak. I didn't want to play chess again for half a year. I had lost my direction. Chess had been so big in my life, and now, deeply disappointed, I no longer wanted it. I had to learn that you can lose a big game, that losing is an integral part of any competitor's life. I had to learn to endure the misery and somehow get back on top. Ultimately I believe that the loss gave me a new and different kind of strength. I wrestled with self-doubt and fear for a year until the next Nationals, which I won and which is portrayed in *Searching for Bobby Fischer*. I learned that success doesn't come without a lot of work. Many dream of being the best and some are gifted enough to have a chance, but to emerge from the pack you must work harder than the others, put in the extra hour, meet the challenge head on. My grandmother likes to remind me, "Talent is cheap, it's what you do with it." I learned this lesson quite young.

Here is the massacre: **1.e4 e5 2.Nf3 Nc6 3.Bc4 Nd4**. This is the trap. It is primitive and I had, in fact, seen it before, but I had forgotten. The idea is that White cannot take the pawn on e5. Virtually anything else is good. I took the pawn. **4.Nxe5??** We cannot always reason with a young mind. I have a five-year-old student in a chess class who is very gifted. He can solve difficult mating problems. But he often blunders his queen. Why? He is not ready yet not to make big blunders. Parents, be patient.

81 Waitzkin–Arnett

1985 NATIONAL PRIMARY CHAMPIONSHIP

BLACK TO MOVE:

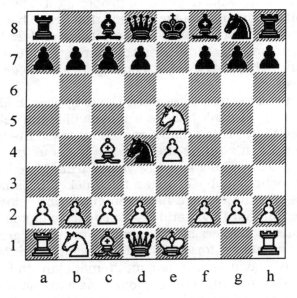

How does Black punish me for taking the pawn on e5?

4 . . . Qg5! The Horror! David is threatening to take my knight and to rip apart my kingside. The correct psychological decision now would have been to castle, lose a piece, and try to fight back. I was shaken, though, and quickly fell apart after **5.Ng4 d5 6.Bxd5 Bxg4 7.f3 Bd7**.

Oh, how I would have loved an endgame now! All of my work on the latter stages of the game and I didn't survive long enough to use it. David continued with sure-handed technique: **8.Rg1 Qh4+ 9.Kf1 Qxh2**

10.B×b7 Rb8 11.Bd5 Bc5 12.b4 Rxb4 13.c3 Nc6 14.cxb4 Qg1+ 15.Ke2 Nxb4 16.d3 Qf2 mate. I never had a chance after my fourth move! I couldn't recover after falling for his trap. This is a reason to be familiar with traps! Imagine losing such an important game without even being able to put up a proper fight. The strange thing about this particular game is that Bruce had in fact shown me this very trap. I have often wondered why I happened to forget it during this game. The fear of the moment? The pressure? A bad roll of the dice? Sometimes we lose.

After the awards ceremony, David approached me in the airport: "I can't believe a player like you fell for a trap like that!" This remark somehow eased the tension between us. It's funny the way life leads us on such a twisting path. The following year I transferred to The Dalton School and David and I quickly became best friends. To this day we have remained very close. The connection that David and I have is surely linked to that day years ago. A terrible moment for me and a great one for him somehow forged a bond between two little boys.

Today David is a gifted mathematician and one of America's top young chess players. As a kid he was consistently one of the best in the country for his age while doing very little studying. And then for years his progress was slow. Perhaps I am wrong about this, but I have long believed that his winning the Nationals as an eight-year-old boy may have impeded his chess development. As a child, competing against less talented kids, David learned that he could prosper while doing very little work. Relative to chess, basketball, piano, tennis, etc., the descriptions of adulation attached to children, "prodigy," "great talent," and "genius," can be a curse. Believe me, success in a field like chess is in fact ten percent inspiration and ninety percent perspiration, as the adage goes. I should add that these days David Arnett studies his chess seriously, and his game is flourishing.

In the summer of 1994, when only 17 years old, he finished fifth in the United States Junior (under 21 years of age) Championship.

This next game was played in Tempe, Arizona, in the last round of the 1989 National Elementary Championship. Going into this round I was trailing Tal Shaked by half a point and needed to beat him to gain the title. **1.e4 c5 2.Nf3 Nc6 3.d4 cd4 4.Nd4 Nf6 5.Nc3 e5**, the Pelikan or Sveshnikov Sicilian. At this point in his career Shaked, as far as I knew, did not normally play this system. He was trying to surprise me, but I felt that it might blow up in his face. I figured that he might be familiar with the main line but was not likely to have learned many of the side variations. As luck would have it I had looked at this variation and some possible traps in it only a few weeks before.

I planned here to set a little trap. **6.Ndb5 d6 7.Nd5!?** I usually played the better known 7.Bg5 . . . but I suspected that I might win this game quickly with a more offbeat variation: **7 . . . Nxd5 8.exd5 Ne7 9.c4 g6??** He fell right into the hole.

82 Waitzkin–Shaked

1989 NATIONAL ELEMENTARY CHAMPIONSHIP

WHITE TO MOVE:

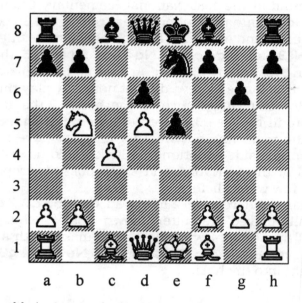

My last move looked innocent enough but in fact posed a dangerous threat. What should I play now?

10.Qa4! and my position is winning. Make the move on your chessboard and see why. I am threatening Nxd6 or Nc7 double check and mate! If he blocks the discovery with 10 . . . Bd7, then 11.Nxd6 is smothered mate! If 10 . . . Qd7, then 11.Nxd6+ Kd8 (the queen is pinned) 12.Nxf7+ and I am winning a rook. Incidentally, if Black had tried to kick my knight out with 9 . . . a6, then 9. Qa4! is the same trap, as Black cannot capture my knight because of the pin to his rook on a8. Shaked could have sidestepped my little land mine with either 9 . . . Ng6 or 9 . . . Nf5, which defend the d6-pawn and allow 10.Qa4 to be met with 10 . . . Bd7.

Shaked played **10 . . . Bg7**, and after **11.Nc7+ Kf8 12.Nxa8 a6 13.Qb3 b5 14.Be3 Nf5 15.Nb6 Bb7 16.cxb5 axb5 17.Bxb5**, he resigned.

You just saw the finals of two national championships decided by pure opening trap. I could imagine how Shaked felt after this game; it had happened to me. He trained all year to fight for the championship, but then the bout was over before he had a chance to throw a single punch.

In retrospect, and I'm sure that Tal would agree, instead of trying out this sharp new opening in such an important game, he should have played the Scheveningen Sicilian, which was his normal defense against e4. It would have been a tough fight, nothing like this game. He was trying to trick me, and ended up getting tricked himself.

I would also like to note that at the beginner level, traps are often not lethal! In my game against Arnett my second and killer mistake was that I didn't thoughtfully try to regroup once I had erred. If we go back to the position after 4 . . . Qg5 and consider the fact that I could have played 5.0-0 Qxe5 6.c3 and d4, we will see that I could have made the game interesting had I kept my head. What is a pawn or even a piece between eight-year-old boys? Often in chess, however, the first mistake is quickly followed by another. This happens, in subtler fashion, to even the greatest grandmasters. It is a human weakness that we become flustered after going wrong. If a competitor can be level-headed in battle, cut his losses and regroup, then he can survive many traps.

A player should also try to get in tune with the atmosphere surrounding a trap. What are the tell-tale signs? If your opponent reels off his first moves like a speed demon or confidently does something unusual in the beginning of the game or makes a move and excitedly runs away from the board, then you should be on the lookout for booby traps. Also, beware of actors! If your opponent makes a move and quickly smacks himself on the head or gets visibly upset, it could be a ruse. Think twice before whipping off the hanging piece. Psychology in chess is a very real thing. Cultivating a poker face is a difficult and worthwhile assignment. You should try to be aware of your opponent's mental state enough to have a clue of his or her mood but not so much that you will be distracted from the game.

I suggest that the beginning student start with a limited opening repertoire that does not require much work. Concretely, I would recommend the two knights with Ng5: 1.e4 e5 2.Nf3 Nc6 3.Bc4 Nf6 4.Ng5. I won many games this way and it can lead to fun complications suitable for a young mind. From the black side I would suggest avoiding this possibility by playing 3 . . . Bc5 before Nf6. A handy reference of opening traps for beginners is Pandolfini's *Chess Openings: Traps and Zaps*, in two volumes.

I cannot stress too much that cheap tricks have little to do with great chess. I would urge you as a beginner not to get caught in the snare of searching for fast tricky wins. Even if you succeed a few times, it will not help you become a good chessplayer. At the beginning choose an opening that is comfortable, and learn its pitfalls. Don't get trapped like Shaked and me, but don't spend a lot of time researching cheap traps to terrorize your opponents. There is too much important chess to learn.

QUIET MOVES IN ATTACK

Relative to other phases of a chess game, attacks are fast. The troops close in, our neat position is suddenly unclear, crazy, thrilling, violent. Nonetheless there is an order to a good attack, a synchrony within the chaos. The master of aggressive play will feel the relationships between his pieces, and will understand the rhythm, the flow, of the attack. It is very hard to overwhelm a strong defense with brute force, and so it is often necessary for the attacker to step back from the battlefield to see what the missing element is; what would make this unstoppable. This is often where the quiet move in the attack comes into the picture. In the chapter on busting open the kingside, as you might recall, in the middle of the destruction of my opponent's kingside, we reached this position:

83 Waitzkin–Berman, 1989

WHITE TO MOVE:

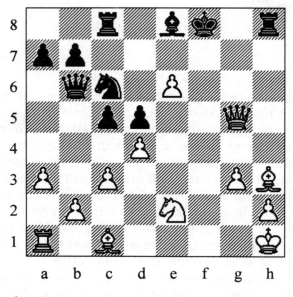

A quiet move makes my attack
unstoppable.

Here I felt that there was an element missing in my attempt to checkmate. I needed one more piece to make ends meet. And so, in the thick of battle, after sacrificing an exchange and breaking everything wide open I simply played **1.Be3!** and the game was essentially over. The entrance of my undeveloped warrior (the rook on a1) was decisive.

The player has to be in control of his or her emotions during a chess game. Even in the maddening rush of battle a great general will keep his cool, plot intelligently, and notice weaknesses in the enemy's forces. Remember that you are not a soldier in the chess game; you are the commander, and must act with detachment and authority. There are many chess players who are incapable of making a simple slow move in a crazy position because they are aflame with the passion to crush their opponent. Desire is not enough. To win we must be better than our opponent, and this often means showing class with a move that seems, to the impassioned eye, anti-climactic.

I reached the position below against a strong International Master in the sixth round of the St. Martin Open in 1993. The basic flow of the game is similar to some that I have already discussed in the book. I am attacking on the kingside and he on the queenside. The game has reached the critical stage and here I must make a decision. I can play 1.Qxh6, evaluating that after 1 . . . Qxa2+ my king can escape and I will have time to checkmate with Qg7 mate. This would be a decision very much in line with those we discussed in the "Courage" chapter. In order to make a move like Qh6 I must calculate all of his possibilities and evaluate that in every line I win. My other choice is to simply stop his threat with 1.b3 and let the game go about its course. This is a *very* hard decision. I ask the reader to try to analyze the consequences of 1.Qxh6. Set the position up on a board and move the pieces if you want to. What is my correct decision?

84 Waitzkin–Thorsteins

ST. MARTIN, 1993

WHITE TO MOVE:

Analyze the consequences of 1.Qxh6.

After much thought, I played **1.Qxh6**. He responded with **1 . . . Qxa2+ 2.Kc1 Bf4+!** A necessary move that gives up a bishop to slow my mating attack. My queen is distracted from the g7 square so Black has more time to operate. I had seen this move but not what Black had in store after **3.Qxf4**.

85

BLACK TO MOVE:

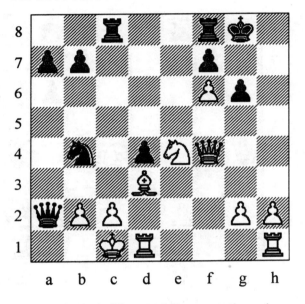

The critical position and the one where I missed his possibility. Take some time now and try to find Black's best move.

In my analysis of this position a few moves earlier I was so involved in the complexity of the position and with the rapidity with which things were happening, I missed a quiet move that poses threats that cannot be met. He played **3 . . . Qa4!!**

86

WHITE TO MOVE:

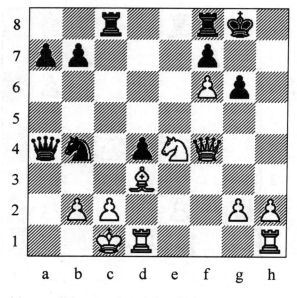

My confidence was misguided.

His move simply mounts more pressure on my c2-pawn. Now he threatens 4 . . . Rxc2, and if I put a rook or queen on d2, then Qa1 is mate. I quickly realized the mistake I had made. It's strange the way things work. I was playing this game in a romantic style that I favor. But this was a game in which my confidence was misguided. I had missed a simple, concrete, and devastating response. I tried to run my king away with **4.Kd2**. I should note that 4.Qf2 would have also failed after 4 . . . Rxc2+! 5.Bxc2 Rc8 6.Nc3 Qa1+ 7.Kd2 Qxb2, and the attack is overpowering.

My king has been flushed from his royal home and is now a sitting duck. **4 . . . Rxc2+ 5.Bxc2 Qxc2+ 6.Ke1**. Here is another interesting moment. How had Thorsteins planned to finish me off?

87

BLACK TO MOVE:

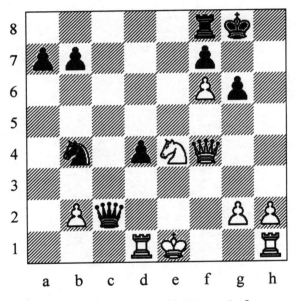

Another quiet move spells the end of Waitzkin.

Thorsteins casually brings his rook into the game with **6 . . . Re8!** I went on to lose convincingly after **7.Rxd4 Nd3+! 8.Rxd3 Qxd3 9.Kf2 Rxe4 10.Qb8+ Kh7 11.h3 Qe3+**, and I resigned because after **12.Kf1, Qe1** is mate.

It is said that in chess we learn much more from our defeats than our victories. I was blushing after this one. Passionate for the win, I was punished for being unable to step back and notice a deadly little quiet move.

15 ZWISCHENZUG

If chess were all straight lines and standard calculation, then it would be a normal game that clever mathematicians could dominate easily. Positions, though, are filled with hidden traps and sharp turns and it often takes a nimble imaginative mind to find the winning way. It is not infrequent that a player will be shocked with an off-the-beaten-path move. The *zwischenzug* or *in-between move* is a dangerous little surprise. Often entire plans and streams of calculation hang on the premise that, in a given moment, a perfect little forced change in the position, or even in the very nature of the position, can take place. Games turn on this very useful tactical device, which I sometimes call an "intermezzo." Consider the next position:

88

BLACK TO MOVE:

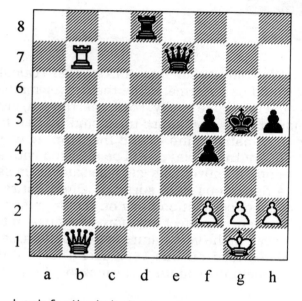

Look for the in-between move.

In the diagrammed position the black queen is threatened. But Black, instead of simply moving the queen out of attack, remembers principles we learned in our discussion of back-rank mates. He proudly plays **1 . . . Qxb7** and smiles broadly at the board, as he has done well. Now White cannot recapture with 2.Qxb7 because of 2 . . . Rd1 mate. Ah, but there is more. White has also read my book and has not forgotten about back-rank mates. In fact, the player with the white pieces has read more attentively and was thinking about this very chapter when he played Rb7. He has set a trap.

89

WHITE TO MOVE:

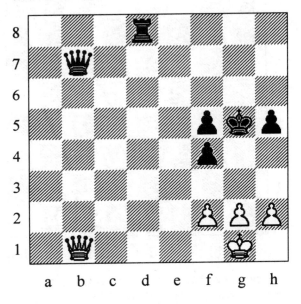

Make the recapture possible.

White plays **2.h4+**, and suddenly Black realizes that he has been tricked! After **2 . . . Kxh4**, the white king has an escape square and **3.Qxb7** is possible. White has won a queen for a rook and pawn and should go on to win the game. Notice that the zwischenzug changed the position, allowing the player to achieve his goal (in this case the capture of the black queen).

The result of an in-between move is not always so dramatic as winning a queen. Often a zwischenzug is simply a little addition to the tactics that helps one side. The next position is a simple example from one of my games.

90 Waitzkin–Lopresti, 1987

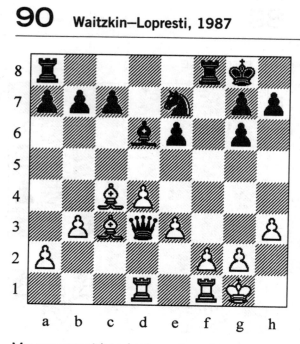

My opponent has just captured my queen with . . . Qxd3. What is my best move?

The instinctive response of many players here would be to simply recapture the queen with either the rook or bishop. There is better, though. I played the "in-between move" **1.Bxe6+**, winning a pawn. Black moved his king away, **1 . . . Kh8**, and only then did I recapture **2.Rxd3**. In this example I simply took a moment before recapturing a queen to whip off an enemy pawn *with check*. This is a handy way to win material; if I had taken the queen first, Black could have easily protected the pawn on e6 and maintained material equality. The pawn advantage turned out to be decisive in the game.

I should note the obvious fact that a zwischenzug better be forcing or else the other guy will not allow the next step of the tactic. For example, had Black's king been on h8 in the diagrammed position then 1.Bxe6 would be pretty foolish, as the black queen would move out of danger. The key was that I captured a pawn *with check*. He was forced to address this issue and next I simply recaptured the queen.

This next example involves a common usage of the zwischenzug that is often seen out of the Dragon Sicilian. I reached this position in the National Elementary Championships of 1989. It is a slightly harder problem. What is White's best move?

91 Waitzkin–O'Neill
1989 NATIONAL ELEMENTARY CHAMPIONSHIPS

WHITE TO MOVE:

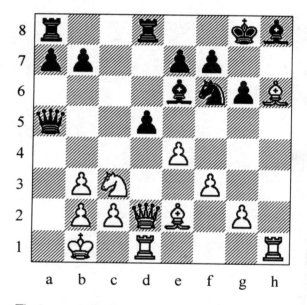

First use a discovery, then an in-between move, to win material.

I played **1.Nxd5!** He cannot recapture with the straight 1 . . . Nxd5 because I have opened up the diagonal on which the two queens lie and could respond with 2.Qxa5, winning a lady. My opponent must deal with the reality of the queens and so, before capturing my knight, uses a zwischenzug of his own with **1 . . . Qxd2**.

92

WHITE TO MOVE:

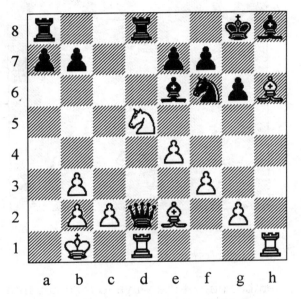

Ah, but I have the final laugh. What was my idea?

People often take the immediate recapture of a queen for granted. I am sure you are learning that it is a mistake to take much of anything for granted in a chess game. I intermezzo with **2.Nxe7+!** and Black finds himself in big trouble. **2 . . . Kh7** is forced, after which I recapture the queen with discovered check! **3.Bxd2+**. Notice how the zwischenzug threw the black position into chaos. After **3 . . . Nh5**, what is my best? (See Diagram 93.)

93

WHITE TO MOVE:

Black was forced to pin his knight.

HINT: Remember one of the ways to take advantage of a pinned piece is to attack it.

I played **4.g4!** and after **4 . . . Rd7 5.Nd5 Bxd5 6.exd5 Rxd5 7.gxh5 gxh5** had won a piece. All of the tactics were in my favor because of the little in-between move 2.Nxe7+!

The reader must be aware of a subtlety at work in this position. Notice that in Diagram 91, my king was on b1. This was absolutely essential for my zwischenzug to work; if my king were on c1, Black would be taking on d2 with check, thus forcing me to recapture. This is leaving

aside the fact that if my king were on c1, then Black's
queen to a1 would be mate. But once again the relevant
factor here for our discussion is that Black cannot make
his original capture with check. The next example ampli-
fies my point.

Here is a position pretty similar to the last one. It has
also arisen from the Dragon Sicilian and once again the
queens are lined up on the a5-e1 diagonal. Let's focus on
the tactic in the last example. Does 1.Nd5 do any good?

94

WHITE TO MOVE:

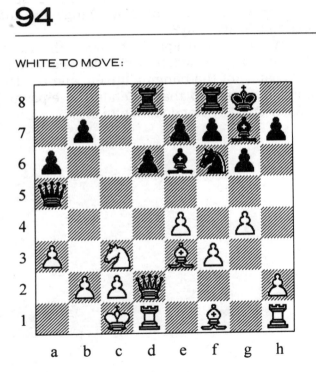

Notice the differences between this
position and diagram 91.

The answer is that 1.Nd5 doesn't work, as Black can trade queens with check. After 1 . . . Qxd2+ White must recapture 2.Rxd2, after which Black can simply trade on d5 and have a fine position.

All right, so the immediate tactic does not work. How can White prepare it?

HINT: Remember my final comments on the last example.

White sets a little trap with **1.Kb1!** Black, unable to imagine that such an innocent-looking move could have venom, quickly responds by beginning a queenside pawn storm with **1 . . . b5?** Now things are different. What should White play?

Here White can win a pawn thanks to the intermezzo that we have just learned: **2.Nd5!!** Black cannot take the knight because of the hanging queen, and the lady has nowhere to retreat to that defends the e-pawn. Black plays **2 . . . Qxd2**. What does White play?

95

WHITE TO MOVE:

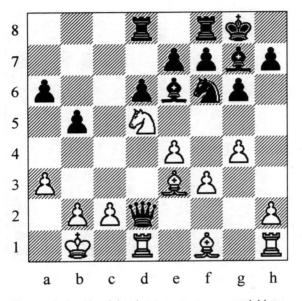

To capture the black queen now would be
a lost opportunity.

This should be old news by now. **3.Nxe7+! Kh8
4.Rxd2**, and White has won a pawn and his knight has
two clear paths out of enemy territory: Ne7-d5 or Ne7-
c6-d4.

To prove the thesis that I have been setting forth
throughout this entire book, "You can take nothing for
granted in the black and white jungle," let's vary the last
diagram just a little. The black rook on f8 has now been
replaced with one on a8. This is, in fact, the more correct
alignment, as the rooks should focus on the queenside.

96

WHITE TO MOVE:

Does the change in the rook position make
the tactic any less powerful?

HINT: Visualize the position after your crucial intermezzo.

Yes! Now after 1.Nd5 Qxd2, 2.Nxe7?? would be a horrible
mistake. Why? What does Black play?

97

WHITE TO MOVE:

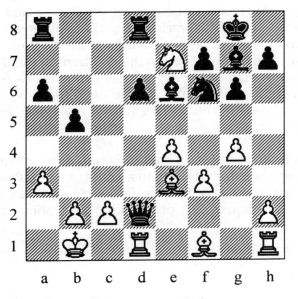

Black's king is no longer a victim.

Black can get out of check and attack the wandering knight with 2 . . . Kf8! Suddenly it is White who is in trouble because he has overextended. White is obliged to recapture the queen, after which the knight will fall and Black will have a winning position. White's best would now be to throw in one final intermezzo to get a second pawn with 3.Nxg6+ hxg6 4.Rxd2, and Black is in the driver's seat.

We can see from this last position that using a zwischenzug carries some responsibility. You must realize that the more elements you take on in a chess game, the more you will eventually have to deal with. The simple difference of a rook sitting on a8 instead of f8 refuted a clever tactic. Instead of winning a pawn White wound up losing the game. Once again we notice the interplay between imagination and calculation. White had a nice idea here but it didn't work! In my chess classes I notice that even my most talented students throw their hands in the air the instant I set up the position on the demonstration board. It is one of the sternest tests of a teacher to impress upon his students the need to think, to consider, to imagine the consequences and take time before moving.

The final example of this chapter is the most complex. I reached this position in a game in a simultaneous exhibition that I gave in New Jersey when I was twelve years old, against five or six kids and about twenty adults.

98 Waitzkin–Chaparian

SIMULTANEOUS EXHIBITION, 1989

WHITE TO MOVE:

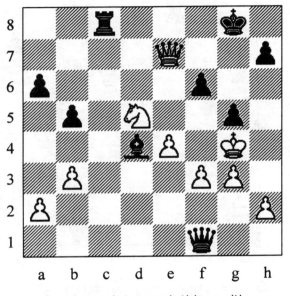

I sacrificed a rook to reach this position and saw a critical zwischenzug that made my position overpowering. What was my idea?

My first move was logical: **1.Qe6+ Kg7**. If he keeps his king on the back rank with 1 . . . Kf8 or 1 . . . Kh8, then I take the Rc8 with check and win, as my knight and queen are too close to his king and weak pawns. (See Diagram 99.)

99

WHITE TO MOVE:

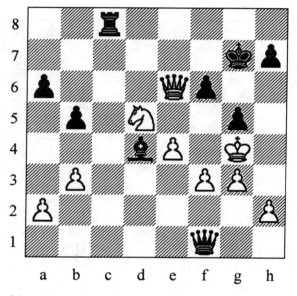

Now came the blow. What did I have in mind?

HINT: First of all, the reader should notice that the immediate capture 2.Qxc8 would be a mistake because of 2 . . . h5+! 3.Kxh5 Qxf3+ 4.Qg4, when the extra pawn for White is very hard to take advantage of. How can I make things more forcing? Take some time.

I had noticed a few moves ago that I had the intermezzo **2.Qd7+!!** What is the point? Black has to deal with the check and my queen still threatens to capture the rook. Let's look at all of Black's alternatives. Both 2 . . .

Kf8 and 2 . . . Kh8 are bad because 3.Qxc8+ is with check and White has an extra pawn and the initiative. Black would have no time to develop a counter attack.

2 . . . Kg6 is the worst of all possibilities. Why?

100

WHITE TO MOVE:

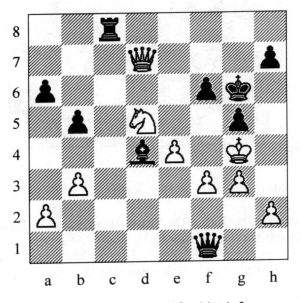

Black had no enthusiasm for his defense.

White can force mate after 3.Ne7+! Kf7 (3 . . . Kh6 4.Nf5+ Kg6 5.Qg7 mate.) 4.Nf5+ discovered check 4 . . . Kf8. Now White has mate in two. What is it? (See Diagram 101.)

101

WHITE TO MOVE:

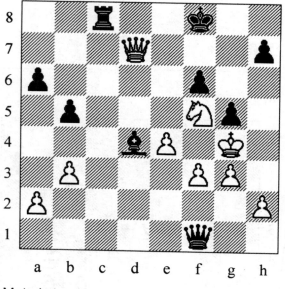

Mate in two.

Both 5.Qe7+ Kg8 6.Qg7 mate and 5.Qg7+ Ke8 6.Qe7 mate finish the game nicely.

Black's final alternative after 2.Qd7+ is 2 . . . Kh6.

102

WHITE TO MOVE:

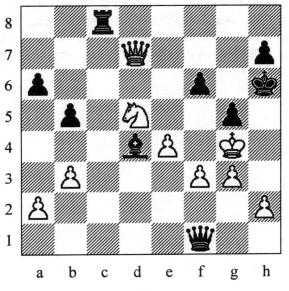

How does this differ from the position
before the intermezzo, and what should
White play?

HINT: Remember how Black generates counterplay if I
don't use 2.Qd7!

With the king on h6 there is no h5 check! So I can
happily play 3.Qxc8 with my king completely safe on g4.
My opponent actually resigned after I played 2.Qd7+, as
his fate was sealed.

In this chapter we saw the power of the in-between
move. It is often necessary to add a little something to

the position before playing what seems to be the obvious continuation. We also saw an example in which a zwischenzug proved disastrous. The juggler's art becomes more electrifying with more balls in the air, but it also becomes more difficult to control. Employing the zwischenzug carries with it the responsibility to be extremely attentive to nuances in the position. We should also be learning by now that keeping an eye out for the unusual will always give you an edge over the less imaginative player.

16 THE SEVENTH RANK AND THE PIG

One of the most important features of a great chess-player is a flexible mind. In the "black and white jungle," you must look very closely to know what is truly there. At first glance you see only a tangle of vines and trees. Stare with a hunter's eye and there is a tiger crouching in the bush, a python hanging overhead. You take one step into the jungle, move a pawn or push a piece. Where is the danger now? With each step the jungle changes shape. A square that was safe is now perilous. A piece that had been quietly developed leaps ahead to become a beast. To survive in this game, you must always look for danger and always be willing to revise your impressions. A good chess game is a great adventure story.

The values of the various pieces are taught to beginners and used by all players. We know that a rook is worth roughly five pawns, a knight worth three, a bishop slightly more than three, and a queen worth nine. This is all fine and good as long as we understand that these values hold up in certain positions and make little sense in others.

Earlier I have discussed the power of the center. Remember how most of the time a knight is more effective in the middle of the board than on the side. All pieces fluctuate in value relative to where they are placed on the board. An advanced pawn that is threatening to become a queen is clearly much more valuable than one still sitting back on its own second rank.

Let's think about bishops and knights. Bishops are generally considered to be the slightly more powerful piece. But all chess masters know that this dictum is strictly governed by place and time. In an open game a bishop will usually have the edge over the knight. However, if the position is closed up, with pawns blocking open diagonals and files, a knight, the only piece that can jump over things, may be more effective than the bishop. Often when a grandmaster sacrifices a piece for a pawn he understands that the piece that he gives away is relatively worthless given its position, or he realizes that the loss of material is worth less to him than the attacking initiative he gains for it. Garry Kasparov is the greatest of all time at understanding the subtle fluctuations of piece value relative to initiative and position on the board. To a large extent this explains why his sacrifices are so deadly.

As I have said, all pieces have their effective terrain. The rook logically belongs on open files. Hemmed in, the rook can be like a turtle on its back. As a little boy, though, I learned of a special power castles could possess when located on the seventh rank. Bruce Pandolfini used to call a rook sitting there a "pig." This is because it can eat up all of the enemy pawns sitting at home on their own second rank. A rook deep into enemy territory can be devastating, to be sure. Chess players, even very strong ones, take this as gospel but rarely if ever offer explanations for this in their books or conversations. Let's think about it. First, pawns are particularly vulnerable when attacked from an angle that they cannot respond toward. In other words as a pawn can only move forward, it is blind to attack from the side or behind. This is frequently the dilemma of pawns confronted along the seventh. Further, a rook on the seventh will often line up to hit more than one pawn in a row.

103

BLACK TO MOVE:

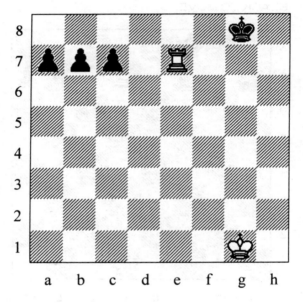

The pig.

If the c-pawn responds to the threat upon it by moving forward, then the b-pawn will fall. This type of setup is free lunch for the pig. The rook can also fork pawns on either side of it:

104

BLACK TO MOVE:

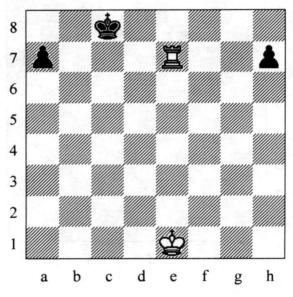

A pig fork.

Additionally, deep in the enemy camp the pig often ties pieces down to defend vulnerable pawns. This can allow other areas of the board to be exploited in the absence of adequate defense. Finally, and maybe most importantly, on the seventh rank rooks impose a terrible pressure on the king, sometimes creating mating opportunities. We'll see this in the next example. It is almost always a violation of one's position to have such a powerful enemy piece inside the battle camp.

I'll never forget one lesson I took at the old Manhattan Chess Club on East 53rd Street when I was six years old. At the time Bruce Pandolfini was the manager of the club, and whenever a guest or prospective member came through the door he would bolt from the board to introduce himself and to speak of the great tradition of genius chessplayers at the Manhattan. One day a distinguished-looking man and his wife came in and began talking with Bruce. They all glanced my way. Maybe Bruce had said something about the little boy moving rooks around a board in the back of the room. They talked a long time, so I put my rook on the seventh rank and yelled "PIG!" to Bruce, who looked back at me a little nervously. This inspired me to call out "PIG" a few more times. I remember Bruce smiling and blushing. Maybe he had bragged about this talented little student of his, and there I was sitting there screaming "PIG" like an idiot. For years I have felt guilty about this little embarrassment to my friend.

Here is an example of a game of mine in which the seventh rank proved decisive. My opponent was John MacArthur, a New York player, coach, and tournament director with a tremendous appetite for chess. I already have a rook anchored on the seventh by my pawn on e3.

105 MacArthur–Waitzkin, 1992

BLACK TO MOVE:

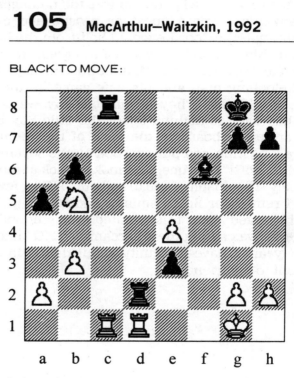

I played one move and he resigned. What was it?

HINT: Combine use of the back rank with that of the seventh.

If one rook on the seventh is a pig, then two . . . Here I played **1 . . . Rc-c2!!**, which is an absolutely devastating shot. The relationship between the four rooks is a peculiar one and should be examined closely. If he captures either rook, I will take the one on the back rank and checkmate. I am threatening, with my seventh rank battery of rooks, to play Rxg2+ followed by Rxh2, etc. I have another threat, though, which I would have put into effect had he played on. John resigned because he saw my response to 2.Kh1. What would I play?

106

BLACK TO MOVE:

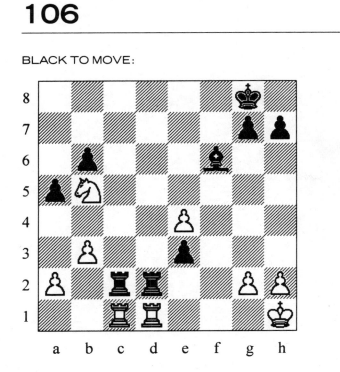

The seventh rank is mine.

Correct would be 2 . . . e2! with the idea of 3.Re1 Rxc1 4.Rxc1 Rd1+! 5.Rxd1 exd1(Q) mate.

We can see that part of the power of the seventh rank has to do with its proximity to the back rank. Being one rank from the king causes some inexplicable hunger to come over a rook. He becomes like a great running back near the goal line. Believe me, even if these explanations seem a little romantic or abstract, *the attacking player wants his rooks on the seventh.*

17 MATING NETS

A mating attack is not simply a mad rush at the enemy king. The aggressor must always have a vision of how to actually ensnare the monarch. If we simply throw our pieces ahead there will almost always be an escape route. This is one of the beautiful elements in chess: subtle crafty attacks are countered by wise and clever defenses. I have mentioned earlier that checkmate is the hardest phase of this game. Your opponent will always be on the lookout and will be at his best to prevent this from happening—he is trying to save himself, after all.

How do you, unarmed, catch a tiger in the jungle? You must outsmart him, dig a hole and set leaves over the ground, maybe stake out a small animal to lure him into the carefully concealed trap. This is a kind of mating net. With stealth the attacker must take all escape routes away from the enemy king and then move in for the kill. Often the laying of the trap involves a paradoxical move, one based upon the principle of "quiet moves in attack." Let's check out some examples.

First a simple position.

107 Khmelnitsky–Waitzkin, 1992

BLACK TO MOVE:

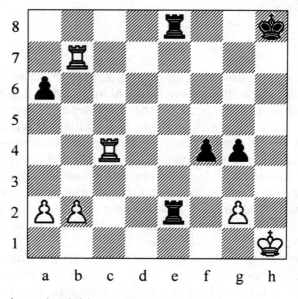

I reached this position in a time scramble
against a strong International Master.
What is Black's best move?

HINT: Net the white king.

I played **1 . . . g3!** taking away any potential escape
route from the white king. There is no way for my opponent to escape the upcoming back-rank mate. 2.Rc1 is
futile because I have two rooks on the e-file and after
2 . . . Re1 +, 3.Rxe1 Rxe1 is mate. My thought process was
simple. I saw that after an immediate Re1 + he could play
Kh2, so I closed the escape path.

Here is a slightly more difficult position. The black king is clearly vulnerable, as he has no pawn cover and my rook and two bishops are bearing down on his position. The question is: how do we take advantage of these factors and checkmate?

108 Waitzkin–Sack, 1987

WHITE TO MOVE:

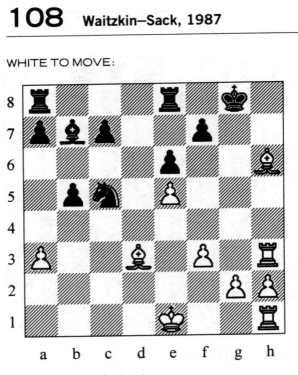

Think of a mating net.

HINT: Figure out a way to reorganize the white pieces so that the black king cannot get away. I have a forced mate in six moves, one of which is a crucial "quiet" one.

I relocated my dark-squared bishop, with tempo, to f6 so that the king cannot escape to the center via f8-e7: **1.Rg3+ Kh8 2.Bg7+ Kg8 3.Bf6+ Kf8**. So far all of Black's moves have been forced, and it is here that I must make a quiet and decisive move. What is best?

109

WHITE TO MOVE:

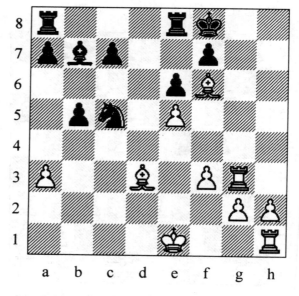

A quiet move wins.

I played **4.Bh7!** after which my opponent resigned. There is no way to prevent mate and after the desperation check 4 . . . Nd3+ 5.Kd2, 6.Rg8 mate is unavoidably next. To set up this mating net I needed a vision of what was preventing checkmate. My 4.Bh7 had the sole purpose of defending the g8 square for my rook. There was one more way to mate other than Bh7. Look back at the last diagram and find a second solution.

The move 4.Rh3! would also have forced mate, as 4 . . . Nxd3 is irrelevant after 5.Kd2 or 5.Kf1. There is no way for Black to meet the threat of Rh8 mate. Sometimes mating just involves a little reorganization.

My next example is more difficult and does not actually force mate but wins a piece because of the threat posed by a great netting move. White and Black have equal material but I have two rooks on the seventh. The power of two rooks on the seventh is often overwhelming, as we saw in the last chapter. I also have an active king, which is good in the endgame as long as he does not come under heavy fire. I made a very powerful move here that forced my opponent to resign. He saw the loss of a piece and, soon after, the game. What was the move? (See Diagram 110.)

110 Waitzkin–Faust, 1988

WHITE TO MOVE:

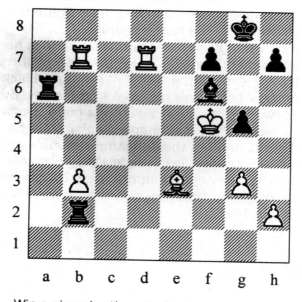

Win a piece by threatening a distant mate.

HINT: Stop all checks and set up a mating net.

I played **1.Bc5!!** with the idea of 2.Rb8+ Kg7 3.Bf8+ Kg8 4.Bh6+ Bd8 5.Rdxd8 mate. 1.Bc5 prepares to take away the king's escape route from the back rank: g8-g7-h6. Let's look at the various ways that Black can try to save the game.

First of all notice that my bishop move disallowed any checks because the f2 square is covered and the fifth rank is blocked. If 1 . . . Ra5, then the rook has left the defense of his Bf6. So 2.Kxf6 wins, as it threatens back-rank mate: My king has taken away the g7 square from his king!

Attempting to guard the back rank with 1 . . . Ra8 is not effective either, as I am simply up a piece after 2.Kxf6.

So that leaves only the option of Black trying to open up a new escape route with **1 . . . h5**. This is an interesting try but it too falls short. What should I play?

111

WHITE TO MOVE:

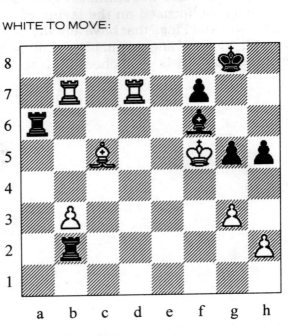

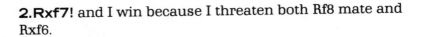

Another double threat.

2.Rxf7! and I win because I threaten both Rf8 mate and Rxf6.

In these examples you have seen the importance of limiting the enemy king's flight possibilities. Often the mating net comes to mind only after the calculation of various mating attempts that fall short. You notice how your opponent is escaping in these variations and so you make this impossible. Nets can take on many different guises and often they are very difficult to make out. Sometimes a crucial netting move takes away a square that a fleeing king will need five moves down the line of a complex variation. When your attacks reach this degree of subtlety your opponents will often have no idea what you are doing and will stumble right into the trap. In this chapter we focused on the laying of the net. In the next we will find kings that have already been snared but are still kicking and scratching. Killing the king swiftly and beautifully is what chess is all about.

18 SAC FOR MATE!

So here we are: you and I. I began this book by showing the reader some simple mates. Just when you got a glimpse of the treasured land I took it from you, said that you must learn how to get there. Chess is like this. As soon as you learn an idea and demonstrate that you can apply it on one level of play, you discover that you must relearn it, or at least refine it, to be able to apply it on a higher level. The game is elusive this way, keeps beckoning us forward. It bewitches us to learn more. It is incredible, really, that chess is so rich.

The great chess players of the world understand the themes of this book to near-perfection. Top players barely have to think about double attacks, discoveries, and the need to exploit the seventh rank with their rooks. They can feel tactical combinations in their fingers in the same way that a great pianist feels the music in his hands. At the highest level calculation becomes something akin to instinct. But we are jumping ahead. It is from the concepts of aggressive play discussed in this book that the fledgling player defines his or her own style. This is your base and you must know it, love it, and then expand from it. Once the basic weapons of attacking chess are securely within your intuitive arsenal, you will go in your own direction. Maybe you'll even stop attacking, if it suits your personality, and become a master of defense like Karpov, who feasts on the attacking energy of the most aggressive players, who busts up attacks and then matter-of-factly collects loose pawns for the win. I have my approach to chess and you will have yours. This is part of the richness of the royal game. The 64 squares parallel the world to such an absurd extent that some forget that chess is not, in fact, life. Your values will become part of your chess approach. Your personality will form your chess style. I see it again and again in chess. Know the man and you can see a great deal of what he is likely to play across the board. But again I am jumping ahead. None of us are quite ready yet to decide if we will play in the style of Kasparov or Karpov. There is still much more work to be done.

In this chapter we will look at some more difficult mates. These positions resulted from long intense battles rife with elements that we have discussed in the pages of this book. In each of these fights, I was winning but I had not yet won. As I have suggested earlier, winning a won game may be the sternest test of all. In these games I was going for mate. But remember, between good players it is unusual to have the result decided by something as obvious as, say, a back-rank mate. Frequently in chess we gain by first giving away. Mating ideas often involve the sacrifice of material that uncovers a weakness and spells unavoidable violent doom for the defender. In this chapter, watch for sacrifices. The first two are simpler. Take them as warm-ups.

I reached this position in 1992 against Luis Hoyos-Milan, a strong master and respected chess journalist. The game had been a crazy struggle in which I was in trouble for much of the time. However, Luis had not taken advantage of his opportunities and in the chaos of a time scramble I wrapped up the game.

112 Waitzkin–Hoyos-Milan, 1992

WHITE TO MOVE:

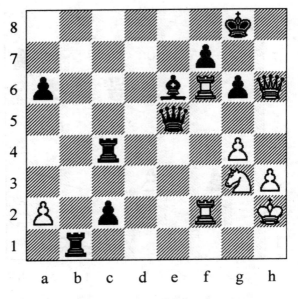

Remember the theme of this chapter.

HINT: Keep in mind that if I don't do something fast I will certainly lose, as Black is on the verge of queening a pawn and my king is far from safe. What did I play?

I have forced mate in two and Luis resigned after **1.Rxg6+!** because after 1 . . . fxg6, 2.Rf8 is mate.

The next example is a little harder. My opponent is a Canadian FIDE Master. I have gotten the better of him in a complex and fascinating game. White to move, but not so fast. Don't move until you see all the lines. What did I play?

113 Waitzkin–Olesen, 1992

WHITE TO MOVE:

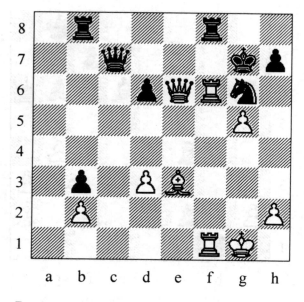

Don't move until you see it.

HINT: No hints this time.

I played **1.Rxg6+!! hxg6 2.Bd4+ Kh7** (2 . . . Rf6 is ridiculous, though it prolongs the misery.) This was the critical position to arrive at when first calculating the position. Did you see it? If not, envision this position from the original diagram and find mate in two.

3.Qh3+! and my opponent resigned because after 3 . . . Kg8, 4.Qh8 is mate.

Go back to the original diagram now and note that there are other ways to win. I am up a pawn, after all, and my pieces are swarming around his king. Also decisive would have been: 1.Rxf8 Rxf8 (if 1 . . . Nxf8, 2.Bd4 is mate). 2.Bd4+ Ne5, and here I have mate in two. You can try to find it by envisioning the position from the original diagram. 3.Qh6+ Kg8 4.Rxf8 mate. I chose 1.Rxg6 because it was prettier and the most forcing. Either decision, though, would be fine.

All right. Now, if you have solved the last two and feel great . . . get ready for a challenge. These next two are from games that I am especially proud of.

I played this game two weeks after turning eleven. The tournament was held in Hartford, Connecticut, in late December 1987. At this point in my chess life I was traveling with my father on the weekends, from state to state, competing against adults in various open tournaments. We were both caught up in the thrill of taking on, and sometimes taking down, serious players who had competed for many years. I felt very free playing in these events, because, in a sense, I could never lose. I was almost always the youngest player in the tournament, which meant that the pressure was on the other guy.

For a 35-year-old man who believes himself to be quite good at his serious art, to sit across from an impatient and naively confident eleven-year-old who zestfully attacks from every angle must be a harrowing experience. Frequently I noticed that the adult not only wanted to beat me, but he wanted to win while appearing as though he were not really trying. I know now that this posing gave me an edge.

In more recent years I have observed that there are several internationally titled players around New York who consistently have poor results when playing against juniors. These guys cross their legs, look out the window at the birds, or go out for coffee and a chat with their friends while the youngster calculates and sets his traps. Then the International Master returns to his chair and moves quickly to show everyone in the hall that he can see in a glance what it took the kid half an hour to conceive and calculate. Next thing you know, the kid is up a knight and Mr. Cool is biting his wrist.

Anyhow, when I was eleven, I was delighting in my situation. The posing or in other cases the nervousness of my opponents inspired me to create bold ideas. Reveling in my ability to make grown men squirm, I was learning how to play attacking chess.

This is the game in which I beat my first chess master, a big thrill for this young boy. I actually beat my second master in the very next round of the same tournament. In the position below I played **1.Re3**, sacrificing a rook. After playing it I looked around to see if my father had noticed. Whenever I sacked material I knew that he was jumping out of his skin, half afraid that I was blundering and half thrilled that maybe I was playing a wonderful combination. Anyhow, I was disappointed to see that my father was on the other side of the room watching another game. While my opponent decided whether to take my rook, I ran over to him and pulled him to the board. I remember whispering: "Watch this." I knew that on my next move, Dad would really sweat.

114 Waitzkin–Frumkin, 1987

WHITE TO MOVE:

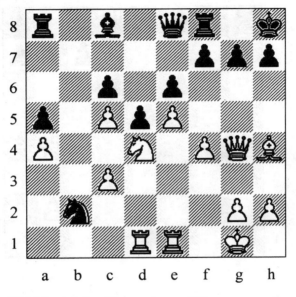

Will Black take the rook on d1?

By now Frumkin was taking off my rook and there were about a dozen players standing around. **1 . . . Nxd1**. It is interesting that whenever someone is sacrificing material players from across the room seem to be aware of it and many come over to watch. It is as if these moves have a scent or a radiance. I paused for a dramatic moment as though I were thinking deeply . . . but in truth there was nothing more to think about. I had calculated this one through to mate. What did I play? (See Diagram 115.)

115

WHITE TO MOVE:

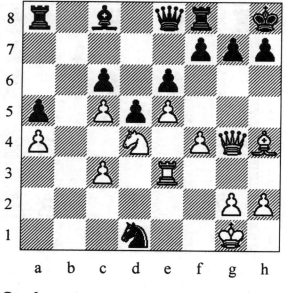

Sac for mate.

HINT: You know it. But take your time and try to see the position out to the end. When I gave up my rook I had a very specific and deadly attacking method in mind. We must not be lazy in a chess game and must think before throwing material to the wind. I have forced mate in seven. What do you think I played? Do not look back at the book until you see mate in every variation.

2.Qxg7+!! At this point both my opponent's and my father's eyes bulged out of their heads as I smiled a little bratty smile. A blast from nowhere! Sacrificing a rook and then a queen; would I have enough material to mate? I saw that I would. Notice the closed center prevents any of the black pieces from assisting in the defense of the king. If you found this move, great job. You might have seen the move but not seen the complete justification. I ask the reader to stop now and once again try to see every variation to the end. This is an excellent chance to both test and train your calculating ability. **2 . . . Kxg7.** What is the correct move?

116

WHITE TO MOVE:

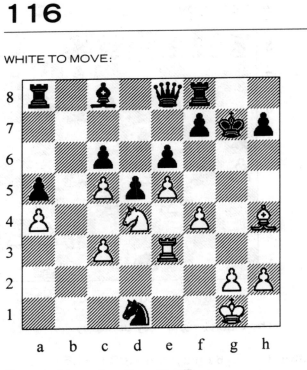

The position after 2 . . . Kxg7.

3.Bf6+! (This is the correct move order. 3.Rg3+ would be a mistake as after 3 . . . Kh6 4.Bg5+ Kh5 5.Rh3+ Kg6 6.Rh6+ Kg7, the attack is no more.) He played **3 . . . Kg6**.

If he had played 3 . . . Kg8 I would have finished him immediately with 4.Rg3 mate.

3 . . . Kh6 4.Rh3+ Kg6 5.Rg3+ transposes to how the game ended. Mate would have been prolonged for one move in this variation.

117

WHITE TO MOVE:

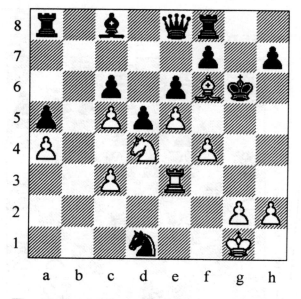

The black king is very unhappy.

So after 3 . . . Kg6 I played **4.Rg3+ Kh6**.

118

WHITE TO MOVE:

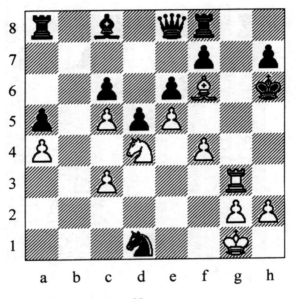

Now to finish him off.

5.Bg7+ Kh5 6.Rg5+ Kh4 7.Nf3 mate! My queen sac had the effect of removing the rock ledge from above a hiding lobster. Suddenly it finds itself with no shelter and must scoot into the open sea with no protection from a hungry reef shark. (See Diagram 119.)

119

MATE:

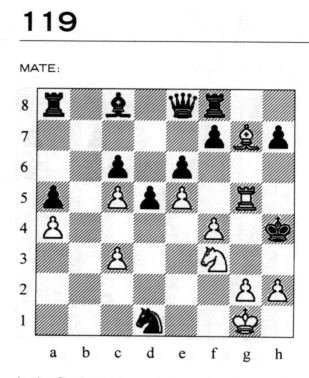

In the final position I am down a queen and a rook!

The career of any ambitious competitor is ridden with obstacles. I have known serious young tennis players and gymnasts, for example, who became good at what they did quite fast and then all of a sudden seemed to hit a wall—they couldn't get any better. All chess players find that certain jumps in playing strength are harder to accomplish than others. There are periods when you study and study and the results just don't come. The chess player goes through a learning process during which his or her results do not improve and sometimes even falter. This is frustrating because the benefit of study is abstract. It is during this time that even the most talented players wrestle with self-doubt and sometimes even quit the game. Then after a while, the player's results pick up. Sometimes the improvement is huge and people begin to notice. Outsiders shake their heads as though something miraculous has taken place. What they don't realize is that this change has followed a period, maybe a very long period, of suffering and hard work. Sometimes the player forgets this as well because often there is a lag between the period of work and the improvement in play.

The hard part of a chess career is the learning, not the playing. Anybody can ride a roll. The real test comes when the going gets rough, when the spotlight dies, the great "prodigy" has grown up, and people begin to say that he doesn't really have it, maybe he never did. This is the moment of truth. The true champion has to work harder just when things seem bleaker.

When I was nine and ten years old people were speculating whether I would become the youngest American master in history. This became a goal for me, and eventually it became an obstacle. At ten I was an expert and during the next two years there were several times when my rating approached 2200, but then I would do badly in a tournament and it slipped back. For a kid, time passes slowly, and it seemed that I had spent half my life with my rating hanging just below the 2200 mark. I just couldn't quite make it over the top. I suppose I feared that I never would make chess master—that at ten years old I had slammed into my absolute limitation as a player.

This was a hard time in my life. My father told me to forget about outside pressures and the great expectations of others. He reassured me that I was getting better all the time but it just wasn't showing up yet in tangible results. He urged me to forget about my rating and to enjoy playing. "When you are a better player the rating points will come easily," he said. "Don't think about your rating." So I studied and tried not to press. I was very lucky to have a father with the wisdom to put these things into perspective for me. Without such a supportive figure I have to say that I probably would not have survived the bad times. He has always been there for me; a shoulder to lean on, a friend to confide in. We are still an inseparable team. Father and son, mentor and competitor, best friends. Our relationship has always been intrinsic to my success.

The position below was from my breakthrough game. By winning this one against a strong seasoned player, Harold Stenzel, I achieved my master's rating. From here the results once again started coming easily to me. It took me almost two years to gain fifty rating points, and then during the next year or year and a half I gained another two hundred rating points to become a senior master. I had to overcome a psychological barrier, and then I was flying.

In this position my opponent has three pawns for my knight. Technically, we are equal in material, but in the middlegame, unless the pawns are rolling, the piece usually proves stronger. I have wedged a rook into d7, a very powerful square. If you recall the chapter "The Seventh Rank and the Pig," the strength of this piece should be more clear. Here I calculated to the end of the game. I want the reader to study this position for a little while. Take your time and try to see all of the implications of the move you like best.

120 Waitzkin–Stenzel, 1989

WHITE TO MOVE:

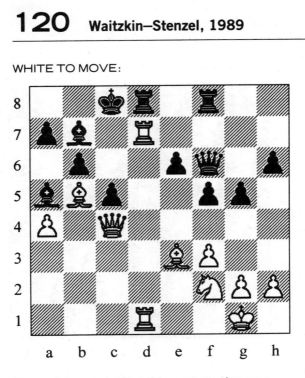

Remember, winning this one made me a master. It was appropriate for the win to be a tough one. What did I play?

HINT: Recall the chapter "Bust." Often we need to sacrifice in order to force mate. Calculate all the way.

I played **1.Bxc5!** giving up a piece to shred the enemy pawn barrier. You might have intuitively felt that this was the correct decision but not seen why. You also may have noticed the title of the chapter and figured this must be right. Either way, it's good that you're thinking. The game continued **1 . . . bxc5 2.Qxc5+ Kb8**.

121

WHITE TO MOVE:

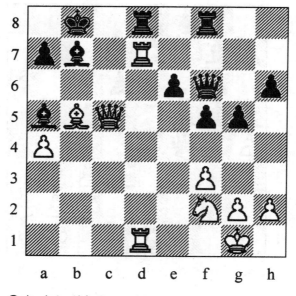

Calculate this to mate.

Now stop. We have sacked a piece to reach this position and I hope those of you who would have played the first move knew what was going to follow. In fact, I have forced mate in nine in this position. This probably seems daunting, especially considering the fact that I had to see everything two moves ago. But chess is a hard game and becoming a master deserves a stern test. Though the calculation to the end may be a bit difficult, the reader might have a feeling what the right move is without seeing everything to mate. This is very good. Often a chess position will be too hard to calculate and the player will be left to the guidance of his chessic sixth sense. Nonetheless, I would like the reader to set up this position on his or her board and to try to find a forced mate. You can move around the pieces if envisioning everything is too hard. Put the book down now and take ten minutes. If you move the pieces, use the diagram above to get back to the correct start. What did I play?

HINT: The move is thematically consistent with the last. Sac for mate!

I played **3.Rxb7+!!** and Black is doomed. But why? It seems as if I have only two pieces, my queen and bishop, involved in the attack. What do I have in mind? **3 . . . Kxb7 4.Bc6+ Kc8**. This brings up a crucial point to my attack. Why do you think he did not play 4 . . . Kb8?

122

WHITE TO MOVE:

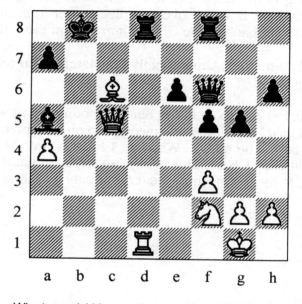

What would I have played after Kb8?

The point is that I can bring my rook into the attack with
5.Rb1 + ! which forces mate. He plays 5 . . . Kc8. The next
move is a hard one to find. What did I have in mind?

123

WHITE TO MOVE:

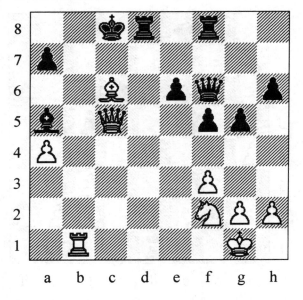

A hypothetical position after 4 . . . Kb8
5.Rb1+ Kc8.

I planned 6.Bd7+!! Kxd7 7.Rb7+ Bc7 (7 . . . Ke8 8.Qc6+
Rd7 9.Qxd7 mate) 8.Qxc7+ Ke8 9.Qc6+ Rd7 10.Qxd7
mate.

Back to the game, after **4 . . . Kc8**. (See Diagram 124.)

124

WHITE TO MOVE:

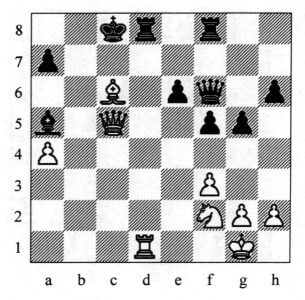

We must solve another little problem. We need to bring the rook into the attack. How can we force the black king onto the b-file?

White plays **5.Bd7! double check 5 . . . Kb7 6.Qc6+**, preparing the final blow. **6 . . . Kb8 7.Rb1+ Bb6**.

125

WHITE TO MOVE:

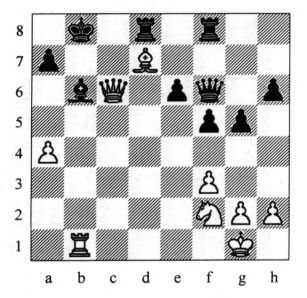

So I have gotten my rook onto the b-file and he has simply blocked. What did I have planned? White to move and mate in three!

HINT: Same ol', same ol'.

Sacrifice with **8.Rxb6 + !! axb6 9.Qxb6 + Ka8 10.Bc6 checkmate!!** (See Diagram 126.)

126

MATE:

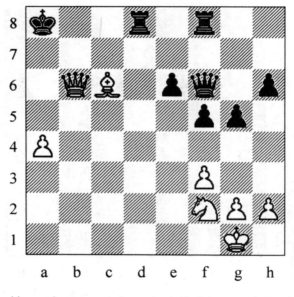

I have just enough material left!

So I mated him ten moves after my original sacrifice. In order to checkmate I sacrificed a piece and then two exchanges. Black could have prolonged the game by one move by throwing in 7 . . . Qb2 8.Rxb2+ before blocking with Bb6, which is why 3.Rxb7 forced mate in nine rather than mate in eight. As it turns out, I could have mated him sooner with 4.Ba6+ Kb8 (Kxa6 falls to Qb5 mate) 5. Rb1+ Bb6 6.Rxb6+ axb6 7. Qxb6+ Ka8 8.Qb7 mate. From the second move of the attack, Black was constantly in check and never had a chance to catch his breath.

I played the Stenzel game in a little tournament on Long Island several weeks past my thirteenth birthday. By the time we finished it was about eleven o'clock at night, and after driving back to Manhattan, it was past midnight. As you might guess, my father and I were sky-high. For years we had been imagining the time I would become a chess master, and here it was, finally. It seemed as if there ought to be a parade, or at least someone I could tell. But it was a cold weekday night and my mother and little sister were long asleep. It was too late to call Bruce. What to do? Who to tell? My dad and I felt that somehow we must share the wealth of this moment with someone. We decided that we would go up to the first homeless guy we came across and give him enough money for a good dinner. Dad parked the car, and we walked three blocks back to our apartment. We didn't see anyone in need. We walked up to 8th Street, about ten blocks from our house, and then once around Washington Square Park. Incredible, a twenty-minute walk in New York City and not one homeless person!

But we couldn't let go of this idea even though it was beginning to seem ridiculous. Then my father said he knew where a homeless man lived. We walked back downtown and into the dark asphalt playground on Houston Street where we usually played basketball, and sure enough, there was a homeless man asleep under some boxes. When I think of it now, this was crazy. We might have given the man a heart attack. I woke him as gently as possible and handed him a twenty-dollar bill. It was strange because the man didn't even seem surprised, as if kids frequently gave him twenties in the middle of the night. I'll never forget the sight of him trudging slowly off to the corner deli on Sixth Avenue to buy his late-night feast. I fell asleep that night thinking about rook sacrifices and this man enjoying his food.

This was a bigger-than-life moment, a romantic conquering of an insurmountable obstacle; I had finally become a chess master. I hope that studying this chapter you felt the thrill and beauty of the sacrifices. For me, combinations involving artful sacrifices are like great music. Perhaps it is through the discovery of very dramatic moves that the beginner starts to appreciate the aesthetic side of chess. I hate it when young players refuse to play unbalanced positions. Drawing a lot of chess games has always seemed like a waste of time and effort to me. Sacrifices often lead to sensational wins, but of course they carry a risk. Whenever you sacrifice material you are changing the dynamic of the position. Suddenly you have something to prove; if you do not you will lose because of the material inequality. With this in mind, work on your calculation by solving many problems; in your games, stretch your imagination, and then don't be afraid to play bold and beautiful moves.

19 GRADUATE WORK

In this final leg of my book I am giving you more difficult positions in which the theme is not identified in advance. This is a relatively practical situation as in a chess game no one tells you when to look out for a fork, a pin, a discovery, zwischenzug, etc. Here you will know there is a tactical shot coming, you just won't know what kind. Of course, in a real chess game no one tells you that a winning tactic exists in the position at all. For this reason one must constantly search for shots. Only so many opportunities arise during a game, and if you miss your chance you may have missed the last train.

The tactics here may be of a slightly different nature than those we have discussed. The ideas will be familiar, but in a different context your eye may not pick out the moves. This is the way it is in chess. All our games are different. The positions we have studied so far are models, not carbon copies of what you will find in the black and white jungle. In one of the positions, for example, the answer is based upon ideas we have discussed relative to back-rank checkmates, but the winning move itself does not involve mate at all.

It is rather uncommon for a good player to dominate a skilled opponent through the use of an isolated theme. A fork does not miraculously appear. It evolves from the position. A discovery is set up with clever foresight and tactical subtlety. Usually a chessic combination will involve several different tactical themes that will roll into the critical position with a building rhythm. A player might sacrifice a bishop to bust open the opponent's kingside, then use a discovery to rearrange his opponent's pieces and finally put a decisive fork into action. The final shot would not have been possible without tactical foreplay. In the upcoming examples the tactics are of this nature. Several attacking principles combine to blow away the enemy forces. You will not be told which themes to look out for and you will not receive hints. Chess is full of surprises. Now, let's look into the jungle with a hunter's eye and see what we can find. I suggest that the reader set up the positions in this chapter on a chessboard.

127 Abdul, K.–Waitzkin

WORLD UNDER-12 CHAMPIONSHIP, 1988

BLACK TO MOVE:

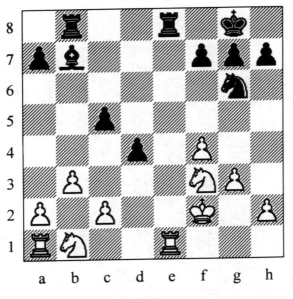

Maintain a flexible mind.

To come to the correct conclusion in this example you would have had to utilize the theme of back-rank weakness, although mate itself was not your aim. In fact, I used my opponent's underdevelopment along the back rank to render his forces completely immobile. My calculation involved first my removing the defender, then my opponent using a zwischenzug to avoid material loss. Finally I made a simple move that involved a crucial principle—preventing your opponent's development. I played **1 . . . Bxf3 2.Rxe8+** (if 2.Kxf3, then the rook is undefended). **2 . . . Rxe8 3.Kxf3**. White's moves have been forced. Now I played the killer: **3 . . . Re1!** and my position is completely winning.

128

BLACK TO MOVE:

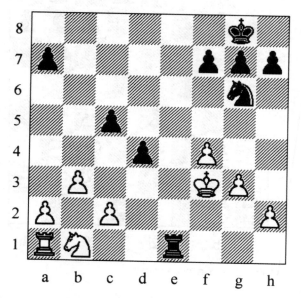

Black is completely winning now.

Notice how the white knight cannot move because of my pin to his rook and the white rook is tied down to the defense of his knight. I simply keep my rook on the back rank and attack the pinned piece. The game continued: **4.h3** (he can do nothing useful). **4 . . . Ne7 5.h4 Nd5 6.Kf2 Rc1 7.Kf3 Nc3 8.f5** (8.Nxc3 Rxa1, and Black wins easily with the extra material). **8 . . . Rxb1**, and I went on to win up a piece. My opponent's forces were tied down by my rook on the back rank. I guarantee this device will come in handy someday. Once again take note of the fact that a basic idea discussed earlier in this book was utilized here in a more sophisticated fashion. You were familiar with back-rank mates, but maybe not with the exploitation of the back rank when the king isn't involved. You must be able to draw these inferences as a chess player.

129 GM Jon Arnason—Waitzkin
ST. MARTIN, 1993

BLACK TO MOVE:

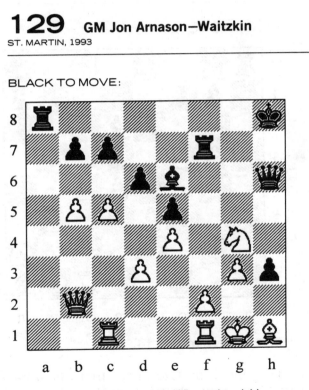

His last move was Nxg4. What should I play?

I have sacrificed a pawn for an attack in this game. After the simple recapture 1 . . . Bxg4? White can simply play

2.Kh2 and I cannot break through. The correct move is
1 . . . h2+!! sacrificing another pawn to open up the lines
of attack. He played **2.Nxh2** and I used the h-file with
2 . . . Rh7, threatening mate. He defended with **3.f4**,
opening up defense along his second rank.

130

BLACK TO MOVE:

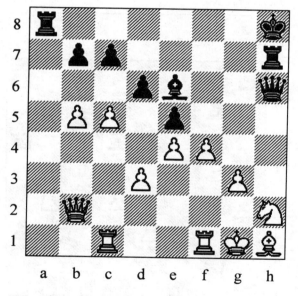

The position after 3.f4.

To play 1 . . . h2+ you had to see that I now have **3 . . .
Ra2!**, sticking a powerful rook on the seventh. The rook
is defended by my bishop on e6 and the white camp is
being bombarded from all angles. My opponent was
forced to give up his queen with **4.Qxa2 Bxa2**, after
which my position is winning. I somehow managed to

throw this game away in a heated time scramble. I lost even after such a nice attack! This speaks to the importance of avoiding time pressure and the value of courageous, resolute defense. Arnason hung on, played resourcefully, and foxed me out of a critical victory.

In the next diagram, I have had a very bad position for a long time against the Croatian representative in the World Under-21 Championships in Calicut, India, 1993. I have defended very carefully and have constantly been on the lookout for ways out of my bind. His last move was Qe7-a7. My f2-pawn is threatened. What did I play?

131 Waitzkin–Bukal
WORLD UNDER-21 CHAMPIONSHIPS, 1993

WHITE TO MOVE:

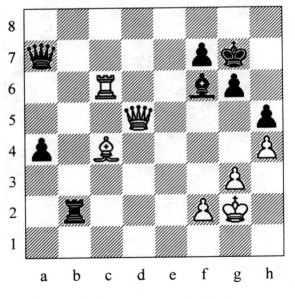

Find a way to improve my position.

When a player has a pressing advantage for many moves and hours, he can easily lose a sense for danger. He has been doing the threatening for a long time and may be lulled into a sense of false security. With my last move I set a trap that Bukal fell into. Now I have **1.Rxf6!!** and my position suddenly goes from much worse to winning. The point is that my rook defends the f-pawn and after **1 . . . Kxf6** I can pick off his rook. But here I must play another little trick.

132

WHITE TO MOVE:

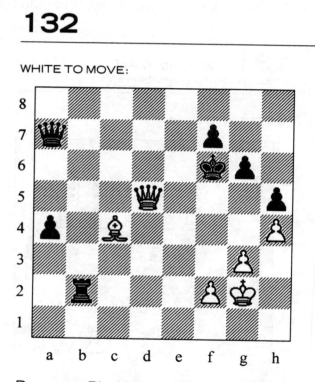

Rearrange Black's pieces to fork his king and rook.

The move 2.Qd4+ doesn't work because the black queen guards the square. Here I had planned the intermezzo **2.Qd6+!** (2.Qg5+ does the same thing), which was probably what he missed. After **2 . . . Kg7 3.Qe5+** and **Qxb2** I am up a piece and went on to win easily. One must maintain alertness when the position is very good. Don't spend the money until you have it in your hand. Your opponent will be desperately searching for a way out, and on the very edge of losing, will often prove quite resourceful.

You remember David, my best friend ever since he beat me in that terrible game when we were eight years old (the "Opening Traps" chapter)? On the next page is one we played more recently in a round-robin event at the Marshall Chess Club. It is my move. What did I play? (See Diagram 133.)

133 Waitzkin–Arnett
MARSHALL CHESS CLUB, N.Y., 1994

WHITE TO MOVE:

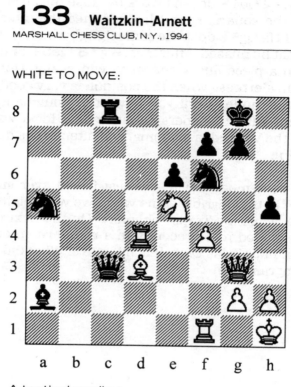

A tactical medley.

I combined the concepts of back-rank mate, removing the defender, and discovery to win his queen. I played **1.Rd8+!!** Now if 1 . . . Rxd8, then the black queen is no longer defended, so 2.Bh7+ Kxh7 3.Qxc3 is decisive. David played **1 . . . Ne8**. Did you see what I would play now? Things haven't changed, so **2.Rxe8+!** and after the forced **2 . . . Rxe8 3.Bh7+**, I win. The rook on d8 was untouchable yet demanded immediate attention. This problem is a perfect example of the combination of various attacking devices to create a killer tactic.

I reached this position against International Master Jonathan Levitt. Take your time on this problem and find White's best continuation. What did I play?

134 Waitzkin–Levitt

JONES MURPHY/AMERICAN CHESS FOUNDATION
INTERNATIONAL, 1994

WHITE TO MOVE:

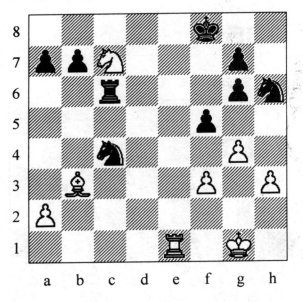

This is a hard one as the solution requires
a patient, somewhat mathematical mind.

Problem-solving involves logical thinking. We can see that my bishop is attacking his knight, which is defended by his rook. His pawn on b7 defends his rook on c6 and can later move to b5 to fortify the black knight.

With Black's next move he will simply move his knight to d6 and be up a pawn. I now combined the themes of fork, pin, discovery, removing the defender, and attacking a pinned piece to win the knight on c4. If you didn't find the solution before, try again now.

I played **1.Ne6+!** If the black king moves to the e-file, then the discovery 2.Nd4+ wins a rook. If 1 . . . Kf7 then 2.Nd8+ is a fork. So **1 . . . Kg8** is forced. Here I played a powerful move:

135

WHITE TO MOVE:

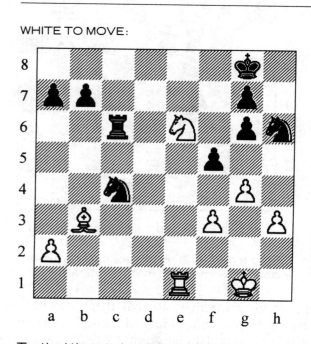

Tactical threats have forced the black king to g8.

After **2.Nd4!!** Black is lost! I forced the black king to a square that would pin the knight on c4. Now I attack the piece defending the knight. He must move his rook, **2 . . . Rc5**, and now I attack the pinned piece, **3.Rc1!** We see a further purpose of my knight maneuver. I am holding the b5 square, so after **3 . . . b5 4.Nxb5!!** wins, as 4 . . . Rxb5 is met by 5.Bxc4+, a fork that wins a rook! If Black does not play 3 . . . b5, then his knight is lost. I went on to victory without a problem.

Next is the most recent game in the book and the last. It was played against the Polish National Champion in the seventh round of the 1994 World Under-18 Championship in Szeged, Hungary. This is your final challenge; take your time and get it right. (See Diagram 136.)

136 Waitzkin–Kaminski

WORLD UNDER-18 CHAMPIONSHIP, 1994

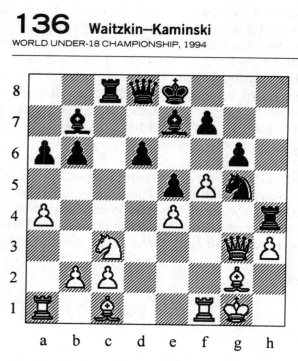

Kaminski's last move was Ra8-c8. What did I play?

The first thing you should have realized is that I cannot take the rook on h4 because of the discovery Nf3 +. The trick is to undermine Black's indirect defense. I combined removing the defender and forks to win material. I played **1. f6! Bxf6 2. Rxf6!!** and suddenly Black's entire game has fallen apart. I am winning, Kaminski's ship is sinking.

137

BLACK TO MOVE:

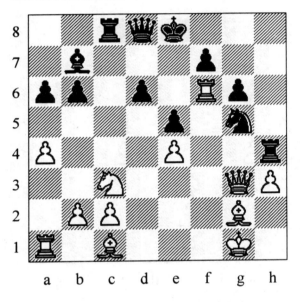

He fires his last guns in a desperate attempt.

If he recaptures with 2 . . . Qxf6, then I have eliminated the defense of his knight and play 3.Bxg5! He is forked, and will lose a rook and be down two pieces! Kaminski played **2 . . . Nxh3+ 3.Bxh3 Qxf6**. (See Diagram 138.)

138

WHITE TO MOVE:

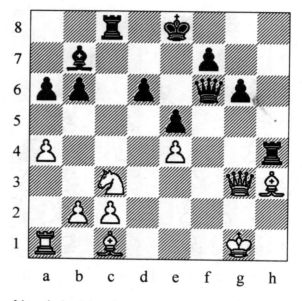

Now I start to clean up.

If you found the first move, what did you have planned here? I played **4.Bxc8!** (4.Bg5 would have been a terrible error because of 4 . . . Rxh3! 5.Qxh3 Qxg5+, and Black is in the driver's seat). After **4.Bxc8** he played the resourceful **4 . . . Qh8** (as after 4 . . . Bxc8, 5.Bg5 would be decisive).

139

WHITE TO MOVE:

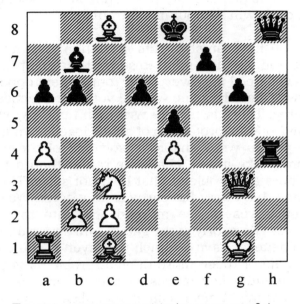

Expect your opponent to be resourceful.
Black's queen to h8 was a good defense.

This was a curious moment in the game. I am up two pieces, a third is hanging, and all seems clear. I had planned simply to play 5.Bxb7, after which I am up three pieces! To my disbelief, though, I found that he could make things complicated with 5 . . . Qh5!! threatening Rg4, winning the queen, and possibly allowing a perpetual check against my naked king. In this line the bishop now must move back, 6.Bc8. But 6 . . . f5! rekindles the threat. The position after 5 . . . Qh5! is still winning but is too complicated, considering my huge material advantage.

I found a way to capitalize on my two-piece advantage: **5.Bg4!** bringing the bishop back to defend. He tried **5 . . . f5 6.Bf3 Qh7 7.Bg2**. My bishop has completed the full loop! I played Bg2-h3-c8-g4-f3-g2 and won two pieces in the process! My position is finally secure, and I went on to win without much trouble.

So you have finished this marathon! You needed a flexible and practical mind to solve these last problems, as you will need it to overpower tournament opponents. Across the board no one will tell you that a tactical shot is coming. There is no one writing hints. Now you are moving from the protection of an enclosed lawn into the jungle. If you were unable to solve all of these chess problems, take it as a challenge rather than a frustration. There are problems that I cannot solve. There are problems that Garry Kasparov cannot solve. We can all train ourselves to see more deeply into the jungle. Whenever I do poorly at the game, I am spurred to study and do better. I have a hunch that even if you couldn't solve some of these more difficult problems you were able to identify key moves, and that combinations of moves that might have seemed inexplicable to you once now made sense when you read the explanations. If this is so, you are moving in the right direction.

I hope that you have found it interesting to read about my chess adventures and approach to the game. For most of my life, chess has been a great joy. I hope that I have been able to convey some of this.

Good luck in the black and white jungle!

Appendix

ALGEBRAIC NOTATION

The moves in this book are given in algebraic notation, a system of recording chess moves that is used throughout the world. In the algebraic system each square has a name consisting of a lowercase letter and a number, with the letter always given first. All squares are named from White's point of view, no matter which side moves. The letters represent files (rows of squares going up and down the board); the numbers stand for ranks (rows of squares across the board).

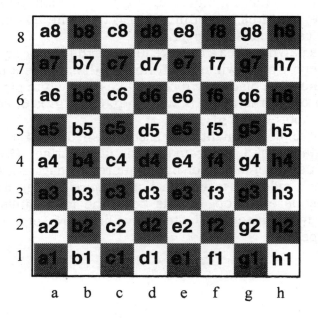

SYMBOLS YOU SHOULD KNOW

K   King

Q   Queen

R   Rook

B   Bishop

N   Knight

Pawns are not symbolized when recording the moves. A pawn moving from d2 to d4 is written **1.d4**. But if referred to in discussions, pawns are named by the letter of the file occupied. Thus, a pawn on the d-file is a d-pawn. A pawn on d4 is the d-pawn or the d4-pawn.

When a piece moves, first the capital letter for the piece is written and then the lowercase letter and number of the square it moves to. If a piece, a bishop for example, captures something on c4, we write **Bxc4**. The piece captured is not given.

If a pawn makes a capture indicate the file (or square) the capturing pawn starts from and the square it takes on. Thus, if a black pawn on g7 takes any white piece or pawn on f6, the move is written **gxf6** or **g7xf6**, sometimes abbreviated **gf.**

If two pieces might have accomplished **Rxe1**, the appropriate rook is indicated by the file of origin, **Raxe1**. Bishops travel on either light squares or dark squares, so each side starts with a light-square bishop and a dark-square bishop. In this book the main lines are given in **boldface**, and alternative lines are set in regular type.

OTHER SYMBOLS YOU SHOULD KNOW

x   capture

+   check

+ +   mate

O-O   castles kingside

O-O-O castles queenside

!   good move

?   questionable move

1.   White's first move

1 . . .   Black's first move, if written independently of White's.

2.   White's second move

2 . . .   Black's second move, if written independently of White's.

INDEX

ABOUT THE AUTHOR

Josh Waitzkin was born in New York City in December 1976. He started playing chess at the age of six in Washington Square Park, where he was discovered by Bruce Pandolfini, who became his teacher. Josh won the National Primary Championship in 1986, the National Junior High Championship in 1988 while in the fifth grade, and the National Elementary Championship in 1989. At the age of eleven, he drew a game with World Champion Garry Kasparov in a simultaneous exhibition. Josh became a national master a few weeks after turning thirteen. He won the National Junior High Championship for the second time in 1990 and the Senior High Championship the next year, as well as the U.S. Cadet (under-sixteen) Championship. At the age of fourteen he captained a team of his friends to win the the National Amateur Team Championship. At sixteen he became an international master. In 1993 he was U.S. Junior Co-Champion, and in 1994 he won the Under-21 U.S. Junior Championship and placed fourth in the Under-18 World Championship in Szeged, Hungary.

In 1993 Paramount released the movie *Searching for Bobby Fischer*, about Josh's early life, based on his father's book of the same title. Josh has frequently appeared on television and has been the subject of numerous magazine and newspaper articles. He wrote this book in his senior year of high school.

Josh's father, *Fred Waitzkin*, is the author of two books, *Searching for Bobby Fischer* and *Mortal Games: The Turbulent Genius of Garry Kasparov*. He has written numerous articles for national magazines. Fred helped Josh plan this book and collaborated on some of the narrative sections.